DONT" FUSS, MR AMBROSE

Memoirs of a life spent in Popular Music

by BILLY AMSTELL

in collaboration with Robert T. Deal

SPELLMOUNT LTD
Tunbridge Wells, Kent

In the same *Recollections* series

Goodnight Sweetheart – The Life and Times of Al Bowlly
by Ray Pallett

First published in the UK in 1986 by
SPELLMOUNT LTD
12 Dene Way, Speldhurst,
Tunbridge Wells, Kent TN3 0NX
ISBN 0–946771–63–4

© Billy Amstell 1986

British Library Cataloguing in Publication Data
Amstell, Billy
    Don't fuss, Mr Ambrose.—(Recollections)
    1. Amstell, Billy   2. Jazz musicians—England—Biography
    I. Title   II. Series
    785.42′092′4   ML419.A/

Designed by Words & Images,
Speldhurst, Tunbridge Wells, Kent.
Typeset by Metra Graphic,
Southborough, Tunbridge Wells, Kent.
Printed by Staples Printers Rochester Limited,
Love Lane, Rochester, Kent.

Billy Amstell
(January 1933)

Acknowledgements

I must first of all acknowledge the invaluable co-operation of Bob Deal (of *Memory Lane* magazine) whose researching and co-ordinating my material has done so much to help me gather my thoughts and memories into usable order. I must also, of course, pay eternal tribute to my wife Tessa whose help and encouragement, not only in the making of this book but even more through our long life together, has made it all memorable. We must also acknowledge the debt we owe to friends and colleagues from these and other days, especially to my old and valued friend Joe Jeanette from our Ambrose days, Bert Wilcox of Zodiac Records, Gerald Smith of *AJEX Journal*, and to Ed Wigley. Many sources have been consulted in the course of writing the book, among them *The Dance Band Era* by Albert McCarthy, *Discography of British Dance Bands 1915–39* by Brian Rust, *History of Jazz in Britain 1919–50* by Jim Godbolt; RAF Museum Hendon; the files and staff past and present of *Melody Maker*, *Jazz Journal*, *Nostalgia*, *Down Beat*, *Metronome*, *Music Fare*; BBC Radio, Pennine Radio and Radio Tees.

Contents

Acknowledgements
List of Illustrations
Foreword

1 Play it in D minor   11
2 A Babe finds 'Guinness Is Good For You'   14
3 Jazzing It Up   17
4 Up West and North Again   19
5 Beginning to See the Light   21
6 'Contrasts'   24
7 'Whispering'   26
8 Early Years at the May Fair Hotel   29
9 Monte Carlo and the May Fair Again   34
10 'Embassy Stomp'   38
11 On the Road   43
12 International Fame and Wedding Bells   47
13 The London Casino, the May Fair and the end of an era   54
14 1284755 in the Royal Air Force   56
15 Sound of Brass   60
16 Flying High – and Low   64
17 'Hello Again'   68
18 With Geraldo on a Wartime Tour in Europe   72
19 'Gerry'   76

20 'When Day is Done'   78
21 Freelancing   82
22 BBC Calling   85
23 'Nice Work If You Can Get It'   91
24 On Tour with Stanley Black   98
25 Freelancing Again   101
26 On The Town and At The Circus   104
27 'Somewhere At Sea'   110
28 A Royal Favourite   113
29 Absent Friends and 'Autumn Leaves'   116
30 'Way Down Yonder in New Orleans'   119
31 Reunion with 'Peanuts' Hucko   123
32 Session After Midnight   125
33 Jewish Party   128
34 Yesterday, Today and Tomorrow   130
Afterword   134
Appendix   138
Discography   140
Index   142

Illustration on following page:
Ambrose and His Orchestra in the Downstairs Ballroom of the May Fair Hotel (February 1933). Left to right: Ted Heath (tb); Dennis Ratcliffe, Arthur Niblo (t); Max Bacon (d); Max Goldberg (t); Bert Read (p); Joe Brannelly (g); Elsie Carlisle, Sam Browne (vcl); Bert Ambrose; Danny Polo (as, cl); Don Stuteley (b); Joe Jeannette (as); Billy Amstell (ts); Sid Phillips (bar).

List of Illustrations

1　Billy when young, aged 8

2　Billy aged 14 with D'Arcy's Baby Band (end of 1925)

3　Billy aged 10 (centre) with brother Sid (standing)

4　Jimmy Dorsey (1930)

5　D'Arcy's Baby Band (1925–6)

6　With some of Charles Watson's Band

7　Bill Gerhardi at Grosvenor House Hotel (The Jack Harris Band)

8　Louis de Vries and his Royal Orpheans (1931)

9　Roy Fox Band at Monseigneur Restaurant (May 1931)

10　Exterior and interior of May Fair Hotel in 1930s.

11　Monte Carlo (1932)

12　Ambrose and Elsie Carlisle at the May Fair Hotel (1932)

13　American 'Blonde Bombshell' Evelyn Dall

14　Part of a Christmas Card from Evelyn Dall to Tessa and Billy

15　A tenor for Mr Ambrose

16　Ambrose and his Orchestra 'Chez Victor', Cannes (August 1937)

17　André Dessary

18　Tessa when Billy met her on the set at Pinewood Studios in the film *Kicking the Moon Around* (1937)

19　Billy and Tessa's wedding, June 1938

20　Tessa and Billy (August 1938)

21　Bert Ambrose

22　Group Captain Basil Embry, CO RAF Wittering

23　Sgt Amstell, RAF Wittering (1943)

24　RAF Wittering Station Dance Band (1940)

25　RAF Wittering Station Brass Band

26　Wartime at the London Palladium

27　With Geraldo's Orchestra in Brussels (1944).

28　On the way to Monte Carlo (1946)

29　Tessa at the New Beach Hotel, Monte Carlo (1946)

30 Billy and Tessa with Sid Simone and wife Dinah, New Beach Hotel, Monte Carlo
31 Peanuts Hucko
32 With Johnny Dankworth, Barry Ulanov and Harold Davison
33 At Bush House: 'Overseas to France' . . . Jazz date (c1947)
34 Band for one of the ORBS broadcasts 'The Amstell Way' (1947)
35 At IBC Studios (May 1947)
36 With Benny Goodman and Tony Brown (1949)
37 Stockwell Jazz Club (1949)
38 With Malcolm Mitchell, Ralph Sharon, Jack Mills and Kenny Baker, the Dorchester Hotel (1949)
39 With the Stanley Black Orchestra at the Royal Command Performance (1951)
40 Tessa and Billy with Kenny Graham and Leslie 'Jiver' Hutchinson

41 Dickie Valentine and family (1958)
42 The Queen dancing to the music of Tommy Kinsman's Band at the Hyde Park Hotel, London (1954)
43 George Chisholm's Jazzers (for The Black and White Minstrels Show) (1960)
44 Chisholm's Jazzers (1960)
45 Souvenir of the cruise SS Canberra (1978)
46 Ernest M. Morial, Mayor of New Orleans
47 The works of Billy
48 Memory Lane Party (1984)
49 Billy and Tessa at home (1985)
50 Billy and Tessa with Flt/Lt Keith Williams CRO at RAF Wittering (1985)
51 Billy Amstell at the Foyer of the Royal Festival Hall (1985)
52 Tessa and Billy with Flt/Lt Andy Delabar revisiting the 'scene of crime'

As a member of the Glenn Miller Air Force Band in 1944, I had the opportunity to meet many of the top British musicians. We arrived in England shortly after D-Day and were to spend the next five months playing for the Armed Forces stationed there. We played a concert at the famous Queensbury Club every Saturday evening and generally stayed over in London and returned to our headquarters in Bedford, 40 miles north, on Sunday evening.

Very often, we were invited to the home of Lady Brown, whose brother, Maury Berman, played drums in the Geraldo Band. A top band in Britain at that time. Many members of Geraldo's band and the Air Force Band would congregate at her home with our instruments and have a good old jam session into the wee hours of the morning!

I had the good fortune to meet Billy Amstell at one of these sessions. He was a charming gentleman, a fine musician and had a wonderful sense of humor. He was a very warm person and a pleasure to be around. It was "friends at first sight"!

In December, the Air Force Band took off for Paris and we spent the next 8 months in Europe and assumed that we might

RETURN TO ENGLAND, BUT WE DIDN'T AND CONSEQUENTLY IT WAS 34 YEARS BEFORE BILLY AND I WOULD MEET AGAIN.

In 1978 I RETURNED TO BRITAIN TO DO A TOUR OF SOME JAZZ CLUBS AND TOOK THE OPPORTUNITY TO look BILLY UP AND RENEW OUR FRIENDSHIP. MY WIFE, LOUISE, (KNOWN PROFFESIONALLY AS LOUISE TOBIN AND WHO HAD SUNG WITH THE GREAT BENNY GOODMAN BAND) WAS WITH ME AND AGREED WITH ALL I HAD SAID ABOUT BILLY AND ADDED A FEW COMPLIMENTS, HERSELF! BOTH OF US FELL IN LOVE WITH HIS BEAUTIFUL WIFE, TESSA, THE MOMENT WE MET HER.

WE HAVE BEEN TO BRITAIN SEVERAL TIMES SINCE THEN AND ALWAYS LOOK FORWARD TO SEEING BILLY AND TESSA. IF THE BOOK IS ANYTHING LIKE BILLY, IT'S <u>GOT</u> TO BE A <u>WINNER</u>!

Peanuts Hucko

PEANUTS HUCKO

LICENSED ANNUALLY BY THE LONDON COUNTY COUNCIL.

DR. TO

The Savoy Direction

IN CONJUNCTION—
THE
SAVOY SCHOOL OF DANCING
AND
SAVOY REHEARSAL STUDIOS
CAN BE HIRED. TROUPES OF DANCERS PROVIDED.
HARMONY HALL
VOCAL QUARTETTES. OCTETTES. &c.. PROVIDED

ENTERTAINMENT AGENTS & PRODUCERS

TELEPHONES: GERRARD 7223.
TELEGRAMS: "DARCEVOI, WESTRAND. LONDON."
CABLES: "DARCEVOI. LONDON."

August 26th 1925

ALL COMMUNICATIONS TO THE PROPRIETOR: BERTRAM D'ARCY, 9. ST. MARTIN'S COURT, LONDON. W.C.2.

Master Billy Amstell,
7 Jamaica Rd,
Stepney. E.1.

Dear Master Amstell,

Re DARCY'S BABIES BAND, you might
mention to your parents that in the event of your appearing
at another hall in the same week you would receive an
additional half salary for each additional hall. As
soon as you have memorized the 6 numbers the Band is
playing and have got an idea of them, you can open.

Of course, you would have to have a
contract from me. Probably you can let me know about
this tomorrow (Thursday).

Yours faithfully

PP. Bertram D'Arcy

D.M.

TELEPHONE: GERRARD 7223
TELEGRAMS: "DARCEVOI PHONE, LONDON"
CABLES: "DARCEVOI. LONDON

BERTRAM D'ARCY
(PROPRIETOR)

Re.ENGAGEMENTS—AN OFFER HEREWITH DOES NOT CONSTITUTE A CONTRACT.

FROM LICENSED ANNUALLY BY THE LONDON COUNTY COUNCIL.
The Savoy Direction (ENTERTAINMENT AGENTS AND PRODUCERS)
also Harmony Hall (for Male Voice Quartettes and Jazz Bands)
The Savoy Audition & Rehearsal Hall (can be hired).
9. ST. MARTIN'S COURT,
LONDON. W.C.2.

April 19th 1926.

Dear mr & mrs Amstell

We have had another
inquiry today for the Babies Band to
go to Australia. We are asking all the
parents of the children, tonight, if they
are agreeable. So kindly let me know
in writing in the morning definitely.
Best wishes
Bertram D'Arcy

1   Play it in D minor

It seems that I was destined to do something musical by way of earning a living, for although my mother had, at one time, to raise seven children on my father's weekly wage of £1, our home always boasted a piano. Little did I realise then how this instrument, plus my brother Mick's alto saxophone and my sister Rose's singing, would have such an influence on my life, or that I would later be playing with the big dance bands, eventually leading my own jazz group and recording under my own name. Certainly I could never have imagined being given many 'plugs' on BBC Radio 2 by Alan Dell, by producer Roy Herbert in his programme 'You and the Night and the Music', and on Radio London by Michael Freedland, presenter of 'You Don't Have to be Jewish'.

My mother and father – together with his mother – came to England from Warsaw around the turn of the century and settled in the heart of London's East End, at No 7 Jamaica Street, Stepney, a small modest house which soon became overcrowded with a family of five boys and two girls. It was quite a relief when an older brother or sister left home to get married, for there were ten of us sharing a downstairs toilet with no bathroom, and the sleeping arrangements were far from commodious. As the youngest, I shared a bed with my brother Sid, two years older. Besides being next to me in bed he was next to me in age too; he walked with me to and from school every day and I came to look upon him as my protector and my favourite brother, although I also looked up to Mick, ten years my senior.

My father was foreman of a shoe factory close to our home. Harry, the eldest in the family, became a barber; Sid and Alf (born after my sisters Kitty and Rose) worked hard at framing handbags while Mick was the only musician in the family before me.

When I was ten years old, my mother and father decided that I should learn the piano and, despite the financial hardship, arranged for a Mr Neville Barley to give me lessons at home. By the end of the first year I had developed lofty ideas about becoming a concert pianist. However, during the second year I began to lose interest in the piano and stopped playing, though my enthusiasm returned the following year and I resumed my lessons. But soon afterward something occurred which was to help shape my future.

Returning from school one afternoon I heard the sound of a band coming from our front parlour. As I listened, the music made a deep impression on me. Mick was the drummer in this dance band and the not-particularly-good fiddle player was Joe Crossman who, in a few short years, was to become one of Europe's foremost saxophonists. I remember that the Chequers Dance Band, as it was called, played a short season at the Richmond Ice Rink, at Lyons Popular Café in Piccadilly and at the Cosmo Night Club in Wardour Street.

At the age of 13 I obtained two certificates at the London College of Music and was doing rather well at the piano – until the day my brother Mick bought his alto saxophone. Whenever Mick left the house without his saxophone I would 'have a blow' and, as I was quick to learn, it didn't take me long to find the right notes. Then sister Rose helped me by singing a few songs so that I could follow her. I have always been grateful to her for the help she gave me, and I recall that my first piece on Mick's saxophone was a song entitled *Dearest, I Love You*.

Before long I was playing gigs (band dates) with Moshe the trumpet player, a giant of a man who, before coming to England had played in the Russian–Polish Army Band. Moshe was in great demand at Jewish functions, especially at weddings, and it was through him that I got to know most of the Jewish folk songs. I realised, too, that many of these songs were in the key of D minor so from then on, when advising musicians how Jewish music should sound, I told them to play in this key. It became something of a joke, for the band would crack, 'Billy says play it in D minor!'

For these gigs I dressed up in a black suit which, together with my best white cricket shirt and one of Mick's old bow ties, passed off as a dinner suit, and I felt like a million dollars!

The evening work proved to be extremely tiring, although I tried to give a boost to my energies by consuming some of the cakes my mother always seemed to have ready for me, packing them into my alto case. In return I usually contrived to scrounge some fruit to take home to her. Although I thought of the instrument as *my* saxophone, it still belonged to Mick, who was generous enough to lend it to me while he continued as a drummer.

I was a small lad in those days – I haven't grown much taller since! – and it was not easy to walk the one and a half miles to the La Bohème in Burdett Road, Stepney, or even the three-quarters of a mile to the Old King's Hall in the Commercial Road where the gigs were played – and then have to walk back home afterwards. Moshe seemed happy to have me around for I was an obedient youngster and was always at his beck and call. He had a peculiar habit of taking his boots off as soon as he got onto the bandstand and sitting in his Army issue thick grey socks as he started playing his trumpet, regardless of whether the rest of the band had turned up or not! Being there ahead of the others I would join in playing my saxophone. Moshe would pay the rest of the band when the gig finished, but not me. On the following day he would call at our house, tell my mother how pleased he was with me and hand over my ten shilling fee, with sixpence extra for 'being a good boy!'

I really don't know what would have happened next if Rose had not found out that a band called D'Arcy's Baby Band was topping the bill at the old Holborn Empire. She made some enquiries and arranged an audition for me, which I passed. There was, however, a snag, for I was still of school age: the leaving age was 14 and I still had a few months to go. Luckily, my headmaster pulled a few

12

strings and enabled me to join the band earlier than I should have done. This was the first step on the way to my career in music that has left me with no regrets, a host of wonderful memories and a way of life that has brought me scores of friendships. Thinking now of those early days I remember that my piano teacher, Mr Barley, was heartbroken when he learnt that I was giving up the piano and taking a job with Bertram D'Arcy as a saxophonist. When I accompanied Mr Barley to the tram and said 'Goodbye', I noticed a tear in his eye . . . he really believed there was a future for me as a pianist.

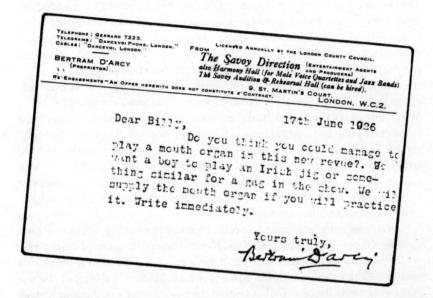

On 19 September 1925 Bertram D'Arcy notified me that I was required for morning rehearsals immediately as the band was to open at the Willesden Hippodrome later in the month. So no more would I be free to help my mother, who was by now nearly blind, with the housework, or run every morning to the baker's for *beigels* and *platzels* – a task taken over by my brother Sid. I had always done my share in the house and had even learned to Kosher a chicken! On 19 October the Baby Band moved to the Rialto, Enfield, and we followed up with engagements at the Empire Kinemas in East Ham and Ilford. Then in late November I worked away from home for the first time, when the band played some dates in Wales. I was a bit reluctant to leave, if only for a few weeks: my family was closely knit, as was usually the case among poor Jewish folk in our district, most of whom were immigrants.

Shortly after the band returned to London, around mid-December, came the news that Bertram D'Arcy had secured us an engagement for the whole of the pantomime season at the Princess Theatre in Glasgow; and so the day arrived when 'The Only Juvenile Syncopated Orchestra in Existence', as we were billed, set out to travel to Scotland.

2 A Babe Finds 'Guinness is Good For You'

The Gorbals, that very tough district of Glasgow, was the setting for my first taste of life north of the border in the professional music business. We played at the Princess Theatre in the United Kingdom's longest running pantomime. The show ran each year for four and a half months through most of the 1920s and its success was due in no small part to that great Scottish comedian, George West.

I shared 'digs' with the band's boy violinist, a couple of years older than myself, at the home of Mrs Stewart in Norfolk Street. This lady, a native of Elgin in Morayshire, was a Christian Scientist and was exceptionally kind and gentle, while both her husband and son made us feel thoroughly welcome. Their home provided a stable background, which was important to a lad of my tender years, and I had great affection for them all. It was not uncommon in this rough district to see men and youths whose faces bore the ghastly scars made by broken glass and razor blades in street fights. Fortunately, nobody in the Baby Band ever came to harm during those long winter months.

For our spot in the pantomime we played popular tunes of the times like *When I Take my Sugar to Tea*, *Paddlin' Madelin' Home*, *Alabamy Bound* and *I'll See You in my Dreams*, besides including some small dance routines and featuring the girls on ukeleles before finishing with the 'Savoy American Medley'. I also recall that one of the girls would dance around in front of the band waving a tambourine with all the natural zest and vigour of a teenager.

It was fun being part of this little band and, despite the fact that I was rather shy in my formative years, I did enjoy the company of the five girls, all of whom were about 15. The other three 'boys' in the band were a good deal older: one trumpet player was 23 and the other was certainly no 'baby' at the age of 30! All the same, seven of us were young enough to need a chaperone and this service was provided by Bertram D'Arcy's mother who did a great deal for our wellbeing, especially when we suffered, as we often did, from home-sickness.

Out of my weekly wage of £2.10s I paid 17s 6d for my board and lodging and sent 10s home to my mother. From the remainder I allowed myself a little spending money before putting the rest on one side. I was saving up to buy myself an alto saxophone because the one I was using still belonged to Mick!

When the pantomime finished at the end of April we returned to London where Bertram D'Arcy secured some engagements for us during the late spring and summer months. However, about a week after our return I had the great good fortune to see one of the top American orchestras on stage. It was Mick who told me that Paul Whiteman had brought his 27-piece symphonic syncopated orchestra for a 15-concert tour (including one at the Royal Albert Hall) and a short season at the Kit-Kat Club at a reputed fee of £2000 a week – a truly enormous sum in those days. I found out that they were playing in London, at the Tivoli Cinema in The Strand; so one afternoon in early May when the Baby Band had no engagement, I treated myself to a seat in the gallery where I sat completely enthralled by musicians like trumpeter Henry Busse and multi-reed instrumentalist Ross Gorman, as well as by the music itself. I was also captivated by the film, *The Big Parade*, a real tear-jerker starring the idol of the silent screen, John Gilbert, and the famous French actress, Renée Adorée.

Alas, times were hard and getting harder, for this was 1926, the year of the General Strike and mass unemployment. Many jazz bands were finding it difficult to obtain work and before the end of the autumn D'Arcy's Baby Band broke up. I was sorry to say goodbye to good friends, such as alto sax player Sylvia Quick, drummer Violet Osbourne, and brass bass player Frank Davies who was to go on with the bands of Oscar Rabin, Clive Erard and Charlie Kunz on string bass and who, in 1984, at the age of 82 was still playing professionally. Fortunately, Mick provided some cheer by taking me to The Saxophone Shop in Gerrard Street, Soho, where I was thrilled to be able to buy my very own saxophone, a new American Conn alto, silver plated with gold bell, for around £30, with case!

Within a week or so I managed to get some gigs both locally and around the West End. My brother Sid had now grown into a big fellow and when he accompanied me to a date on which I was standing in for Mick, as sometimes happened, it was not uncommon for him to be mistaken for the sax player – that is, until I took my alto from its case and had a blow. Right from the start, despite my youth, the rest of the band treated me as one of them. On the first gig, as we adjourned to the local in the interval, one of the band asked me what I was drinking? I remembered my mother once saying to me, 'Guinness is good for you', so a Guinness it had to be. Not being used to such adult pleasures, my head was spinning like a top when I returned to the bandstand. Luckily big Sid held me steady until the alcoholic effect wore off and I could settle down again.

Throughout my career I have never neglected to practise my instrument, and during those early years, even on bus journeys to and from Archer Street (which one had to visit to obtain work), I would go through the motions of perfecting double and triple tonguing. For the double I would say to myself 'Sophie Tucker, Tucker, Tucker, Tucker' and for the triple 'Tu-Tu-Ka, Tu-Tu-Ka' and so on. It was an exercise that fascinated me, and its usefulness was demonstrated many years later on a TV date for George Chisholm when playing the *Spanish Gypsy Dances* at a fast tempo which required double tonguing. I recall Tommy McQuater, our trumpet man, asking, 'Where did you learn to do that?' On another occasion, when doing a TV date with bandleader Jack Payne, the horn player, Jim Buck, Snr and I played a variation on *Carnival of Venice* during a break and simply for the fun of it. He began playing the tune while I triple tongued up and down; then as we reversed the process the 'gipsies' (violin players) in the orchestra giggled.

In the autumn of 1927 I signed a contract with band leader Eddie Gordon to play in Julian Wylie's production of *Gay Dogs*, a 'cabaret revue' at the King's Theatre, Southsea. I was paid £7.10s a week, three times what I had been paid less than two years previously in Glasgow! Our combination consisted of three reeds, two brass and two rhythm, with Eddie leading 'The Finest Exponents of Syncopated Symphonic Melody'. Shades of Paul Whiteman – but that was the billing we were given.

3 Jazzing It Up

At the end of 1927 Mick was playing with Herman Darewski, and he got me a job as sixth saxophonist. On New Year's Eve we began playing a number of Sunday League Concerts, as they were called. These took us to most of the variety theatres in and around London, including the Palladium, the Alhambra and the Empires in Hackney and Fulham. On week-nights we played for dancing at Olympia, from where we did the occasional broadcast besides providing the music for the Tuesday and Saturday *thé dansant*.

The Herman Darewski band was both popular and very large, having no less than ten brass, six reeds and two pianos. Harry Green, one of the two pianists, a good technician with a sound knowledge of music theory but hardly jazz inclined, was Darewski's right-hand man who always addressed him as 'guv'. Looking back I think it was a pretty comic outfit – large and loud. It sounded like a nightmare to me! The lead alto, by name of Freitag, disliked me intensely because with all that noise going on in the band I would frequently 'jazz it up' and sometimes he caught me at it – and then I did it more to annoy him. Later I was sorry I had upset him like that, because I learnt that he had a silver plate in his head as a result of having been shot down as a pilot in the Royal Flying Corps in the Great War.

At the Sunday League Concerts Darewski would introduce some of the chaps in the band to the audience, and we would take a bow. It was some kind of attraction I suppose, for we performed on a bare stage, no 'props' or costumes being allowed because of the laws then in force relating to Sunday entertainment. As I was the youngest in the band, he introduced me as 'Baby Austin' – after the popular economy car of the period – and this would cause a laugh as I was not much taller standing up than sitting down!

Mick would disappear during the band intervals at Olympia. As I say, he was a handsome fellow, liked by all who knew him, especially the girls with whom he would usually be found at break-time! I was on my own then, apart from the occasional chat with Harry Green, so I took to wandering round the sideshows. It was there that I met the so-called 'tallest man in the world', a former deputy sheriff from Texas, who stood well over eight feet tall. When we first met he greeted me with, 'Hello, kleiner' (Jewish for 'little one'), so I knew he was Jewish and I guess I didn't exactly look like a Gentile to him! I noticed the ring on his finger bearing the Star of David, and as we shook hands his seemed so huge that mine got lost. We became friendly, sometimes travelling together to the West End on an open top bus, as it had to be, on the upper deck. Folk at Olympia became so used to seeing

17

us going around together that if they couldn't see me with him they thought I must be standing behind him!

In January the Herman Darewski orchestra recorded four titles for Columbia, all of which were rejected, and I was not at all surprised! The next month Mick left to return to the Popular Café in Piccadilly, while I stayed on to play some dates with Darewski at the Royal Opera House where, I believe, he was the first band to play for dancing. A band much more to my liking, however, was the coloured American jazz outfit led by Leon Abbey which played opposite us at Olympia. I loved to listen to them and took every opportunity to do so, and when the season came to an end at Olympia Leon invited me to play with him a couple of weeks. He told me that he had been engaged by Mrs Kate Meyrick, the 'Queen of the Night Clubs', who owned a number of night-spots in and around London, notably the '43 Club, the Deauville and the Ace of Spades at Hook just off the Kingston Bypass.

I was pleased to accept Leon's invitation and on a date at the Deauville one evening alto sax player Bobby Davis walked in. Bobby, a one-time member of the California Ramblers and The Hot Five, was then playing with the Cambridge University educated Spanish–American bandleader Fred Elizalde. After listening to us for 20 or 30 minutes Bobby passed me a message which said: 'How would you like to join Fred Elizalde?' From that moment I could barely keep an eye on my music: certainly I didn't give another thought to the fancy dancer on the floor-show! To me Fred Elizalde was the jazz King. When I got off the stand I telephoned him and we fixed to meet at a rehearsal. When I arrived, multi-reed instrumentalist Max Farley, the famous jazz bass saxophonist Adrian Rollini, and his tenor playing brother Arthur, all greeted me – and so too did a big disappointment. Although Bobby Davis did his best to get me the job, Philip Buchel beat me to it. I played like Jimmy Dorsey that day, but I am uncharitable enough to think that it was because Philip could dance as well. Elizalde was about to go on tour and a musician/dancer would be a definite asset. I know that the blow was so big that I thought about taking up dancing on the side! Trumpeter Norman Payne tried to console me – but as the saying goes, worse things happen at sea, and I soon got over the blast to my pride.

Fortunately, somebody else had heard my playing . . .

4 Up West and North Again

That somebody was Charles Watson, whose band was making an impact on London's night life in the spring of 1928. I joined him at the end of April, when we began a month's engagement in the Piccadilly Hotel where the beautiful restaurant greatly impressed me. I was excited to be working my first West End hotel with the best band I had so far played in. I remember that the first class cabaret included the Co-Optimists featuring Stanley Holloway and David Burnaby, and during the late afternoon music was provided by the famous De Groot Trio. Later we moved into the popular Café Anglais for a fortnight and followed that with a month at the equally popular Kit-Kat Club.

In early autumn Watson obtained a residency at the largest ballroom in the United Kingdom – Green's Playhouse in Glasgow. He may not have been the greatest alto player but he had a keen eye for business, a fresh clean-cut appearance and a pleasant manner– all essentials for a bandleader. I liked him; in fact, I cannot recall ever disliking any leader I have worked with.

Les Watson completed the reeds while the third brother, Ted, was in the brass section with Charlie Muir and Jimmy Lonie. These were the days of the brass bass, and Bill Cousins, a former Southampton policeman and later committee member of the London branch of the Musicians' Union, played the sousaphone. Norman Pont was on piano with Canadian Bill Cottenden, whose rich Canadian accent always fascinated me, on drums. I believe I was the only 'virgin' alto player in the country on this, my second trip to Scotland, and Mick asked 'Tiddler' Knowles, our banjo player, to keep an eye on me.

Green's Playhouse was managed by Captain Pickering, a tall upright figure with a fair moustache – a typical 'officer and gentleman'. His head dancing instructor was a Mr Gillespie, a Glaswegian with a sparse frame topped by a bald head and a ruddy complexion. I never saw him out of his 'tails'. Les Watson left the band within a few months and was replaced on tenor by Jack Chapman, who later moved on to become Musical Director of Warren's Ballroom – also in Glasgow. Jack held that position for more than 20 years. When I invited him to a Stanley Black broadcast many years later, he told me that he had hoped the job was going to become a regular one! On busy nights Green's Playhouse could become quite a tough joint, and at such times, David Lamb, the 'bouncer' with long razor-slashed scars on his cheek, would keep a watchful eye on me as I made my way to the bandroom.

In Glasgow the young enthusiastic jazz musicians would meet at two venues, Green's Playhouse and the music shop belonging to Louis Freeman, himself a fine pianist and Musical Director to the Walter Donaldson shipping line. At the shop, Louis's niece Hannah kept the boys up to date with the latest American record releases, such as those by the Dorsey Brothers, Joe Venuti, Miff Mole and Red Nichols. Over at Green's, alto man Izzy Duman (who later married Hannah), tenor man Benny Winestone, pianist Billy Munn, and guitarist Alan Ferguson, frequently sat in the balcony listening to our band, and during the interval would chat with us over a cup of tea.

In the summer of 1929 Fred Elizalde brought his band to the Plaza Ballroom in Glasgow. I paid them a visit and felt very bucked that these stars remembered me. Bobby Davis, Norman Payne, violinist Ben Frankel, and alto player Harry Hayes, all gave me a friendly greeting. Adrian Rollini offered me a drink, which I declined as I had been a teetotaller since the episode with the Guinness. I could see that Max Farley – the first saxophonist to double on flute – was 'well lit', with a bottle of Scotch poking out of his coat pocket. I was up in the clouds and even Alec Fryer, the resident band leader, gave me a smile of recognition.

We found very little to do in Glasgow on a Sunday, for in those days not even the cinemas were open. Nevertheless, we were always sure of a welcome at the Jewish Institute in Portland Place, where we enjoyed a warm and intimate atmosphere and where many of the visiting bands dropped in for refreshment, whether or not all the boys were Jewish.

There was, I'm afraid, no such atmosphere on my first Sunday walk down Argyle Street, for I saw Protestants and Catholics moving menacingly towards each other, brandishing broken bottles. I did not stay to witness the bloody outcome but ran for my life. I was told later that what I had seen was a weekly occurrence, so from then on Argyle Street was not on my route for a Sunday morning stroll!

Happier memories are of boat trips up the Clyde with some of my fellow musicians, visiting such beautiful spots as Dunoon, Rothsay and Saltcoats. I recall that on one occasion Billy Munn brought a gramophone along with his favourite record, the Ben Pollack version of *Buy, Buy for Baby*, including 24 bars played by the young Benny Goodman. Our little group would sit around listening to that clarinet without so much as a whisper to break the spell.

Some five weeks before the engagement at Green's Playhouse ended, Charles and Ted Watson returned to London leaving me in charge. Charles and I got on well together, and although I was the youngest member of the band I believe he thought I was the most competent. During this period we broadcast two 30-minute programmes a week. Had I known about 'plug money' I could have made quite a nice little bit on the side. No wonder the song pluggers treated me to tea and cakes! I reckoned I could play well enough but, sad to say, I did not possess any business acumen.

After more than 18 months at Green's it was time to return to London . . . and home.

5 Beginning to See the Light

On my return from Glasgow I settled down well, practising the alto and becoming attached to the clarinet. I played then the Simple System, and was influenced by listening to Jimmy Dorsey and Benny Goodman. I went often to Archer Street where I managed to get a few gigs and became quite well known. I would hear chaps say, 'There goes Mick Amstell's kid brother!'

Near the end of April 1930 Mick took me to see American bandleader Jack Harris who was putting a band into the Grosvenor House Hotel, and after a brief chat I was asked to audition that night at the Embassy Club where Jack already had a band. When I arrived at the rear entrance, well ahead of time, the doorman advised me that the band had not yet come off the stand and suggested that I take a stroll for half an hour or so. As I was 'window shopping' in Bond Street a rather attractive young lady approached me and said softly, 'Hello darling'. I replied rather naïvely, 'Do I know you?' She paused and then hissed, 'Eff orf!' I didn't walk alone at night in Bond Street for quite a while!

On entering the Embassy Club I was most impressed by the décor and the sumptuous furnishings. I was not used to being in such fashionable surroundings. As I unpacked my instruments Jack Harris came and called me to the stand . . . first chorus ensemble then to the second chorus, and as no one appeared to be playing I assumed that because I was being auditioned it was all up to me, so off I soloed, jazzing the tune for a whole chorus. I was enjoying myself and the rhythm section was a delight. This routine was repeated for at least an hour until Abe Aaronson, Jack's partner and the band's alto player, tactfully informed me that the second chorus should have been played on the baritone sax. Well, I didn't have a baritone, but I got the job!

We opened at the Grosvenor House under the leadership of Bill Gerhardi, a South African and a cousin of Al Bowlly. Arthur Niblo and Jock Fleming were in the brass section while I was in the reeds with Jack Marsh and Leslie Norman. Bill Harty was the drummer, and on piano Dave Kaye who in the middle thirties was to form one half of the 'Tiger Ragamuffins' (the other half was Ivor Moreton) who became especially famous and popular with Harry Roy. We recorded some 50 numbers for Decca in the early part of 1931, and while still with Harris I also recorded with Roy Fox who was then Decca's Musical Director of all light music. Hereabouts I was conveying messages between Bill Gerhardi, who was not recording with us – a lousy fiddler anyway, I thought – and his cousin Al Bowlly who was providing the 'vocal refrains' for Fox at Decca. I figured that these two were not all that fond of each other since the messages were always uncomplimentary and consisted of such endearments as 'Drop dead!' and 'Get stuffed!'.

During this same period Henry Hall, who was at the time resident at the Gleneagles Hotel in Perthshire, travelled down to London to record at Decca's Chelsea studios with a pickup band of which I was a member. Henry became a bandleader early in 1924 when he fronted a six-piece group at Gleneagles, from where he made his first broadcast that June. It was arranged that the recording sessions should take place on Sundays so that Henry could meet his commitments to the hotel management – three Sundays in all, during which we cut a total of 12 titles. On these dates Henry was accompanied by Burton Gillis, his fine saxophonist and arranger whose large frame dwarfed mine as I sat beside him in the reed section. What a great guy and what a pleasure it was to work with him.

One night in particular at the Grosvenor House stands out very clearly in my mind. This was during the Depression and a group of Welsh miners, who had walked all the way to London, made their way along Park Lane singing as only Welshmen can. As they were about to pass the hotel, the Italian manager, Pastori, went into the street and invited them inside to sing for the well-heeled patrons. Their performance received a great ovation and they were given a well-deserved meal. The occasion provided a stark contrast to the usual entertainment in the restaurant. We were a typical society band of the 1930s, playing sweet music in a rather sedate manner, as required by the management, under soft lights in elegant surroundings. My basic pay as second alto was £10 a week, rising to £12 at the end of February 1931, when I became first alto, plus £3 for a weekly broadcast – which alone was worth more than the weekly wage of the average working man at that time.

I always enjoyed the cabaret at Grosvenor House. It included the Four Wiere Brothers from Germany, whose act had a little of everything – singing, dancing, clowning and playing the violin. Another of my favourite acts was Giovanni, a performer so expert at removing customers' wallets and wrist watches without their realising it that I have never since seen so deft a 'pickpocket'. His talent was truly amazing.

Before the summer of 1930 came to an end Bill Gerhardi was fired and violinist Hugo Rignold was appointed by Jack Harris to inject some much needed new life into the band. I sensed that I was growing up – musically rather than physically! – and that my playing was improving all the time. At the end of the year Hugo Rignold left to take up another appointment and Harris reinstated Gerhardi as leader.

Because of Gerhardi's swarthy appearance the band jokingly referred to him as 'the Black Prince'. There was nothing malicious about it although we were careful not to use it in his hearing for he could sometimes be quite touchy, possibly as a result of recurrent attacks of the malaria he had contracted in his native South Africa. However, one night on the bandstand I was not in a very good humour myself and certainly not careful enough when he pulled me up over something in my attitude which displeased him. I turned aside and muttered something to the effect that 'the Black Prince is having a go at me tonight . . .' which he heard and reported to Jack Harris. Harris did not appreciate my remarks and this time it was Gerhardi who did the firing! I made my exit from the Grosvenor House Hotel on 17 May 1931, in the knowledge that Bill Gerhardi was more important to the management than I was.

On the credit side I had celebrated my first year at Grosvenor House – in fact it lasted a little longer than that – by treating myself to a brand new Singer Jnr car, chosen for me by Sid. As I couldn't drive at the time he would wait for me near the side entrance of the hotel and give me a driving lesson on the way home to the East End – with his young wife, Sadie, asleep on the back seat. It was always around two in the morning. I was lucky to have such a brother, for nothing was too much trouble for Sid so far as I was concerned.

6 'Contrasts'

One day in the early spring of 1930 I was in Selmer's Music Shop trying out a new alto model and playing a piece from a record I had heard. Spontaneously I went into eight or sixteen bars of the Eddie Lang recording of *Freeze and Melt* with Jimmy Dorsey the soloist. It was a lovely alto and I was thoroughly enjoying playing when Ben Davis, one time leader of the Carlton Hotel Dance Band, came out of his office and asked me if I would like to meet Jimmy Dorsey, who was playing over here at the Kit-Kat Club with the Ted Lewis band.

I was in a daze, for to me as to most British saxophonists, Jimmy Dorsey was 'the King' and we all tried to emulate his masterly technique and polished sound. Pulling myself together I mumbled 'How d'you do?' and 'Pleased to meet you' as Jimmy extended his hand and said, 'Nice work, kid'. For a moment I was struck dumb and all I could think of saying was – 'Do you give lessons?' At 18 I was not exactly a man of the world. On the other hand, I could recognise and name almost every American instrumentalist on records.

Like many musicians, Jimmy Dorsey was up to a lark but never up with it – as I discovered when he invited me to his flat in Bloomsbury shortly after that first meeting. As soon as I arrived, around lunchtime, Jimmy, still in his dressing gown, went to the sideboard and poured himself a large whisky and offered me one, which I declined. He then opened his alto case saying, 'Have a go and enjoy yourself.' I was starry eyed for there was Jimmy Dorsey's own alto and clarinet – on which I did have a go and did enjoy myself! Then he went off to get dressed and returned some minutes later with a clarinet studded with paste diamonds, a present to him, so he said, from the celebrated clarinettist Boyd Senter. As I feasted my eyes on the instrument I tried to imagine the effect that would be produced with just one spotlight on it and the stage otherwise blacked out. I didn't play that one but simply remarked how attractive it must have looked played on stage in such a setting – to which Jimmy encouragingly replied – 'You do just that, kid, when you grow up.'

I remember the day when Jimmy recorded four titles at Decca – *I'm Just Wild About Harry*, *After You've Gone*, *Tiger Rag* and *St Louis Blues* – with Spike Hughes and His Three Blind Mice., The session was something of a disaster, for pianist Arthur Young failed to show up and Claude Ivy, the studio manager, gallantly stood in but was unfortunately no top liner, while the guitarist Alan Ferguson was a great talker but certainly not a great player (to hear him play . . . it shouldn't happen to a dog!). I accompanied a somewhat disappointed Jimmy Dorsey back to his flat, only to find it empty – no wife and so far as could be seen, no food. He was starving so I volunteered to cook for him if we could find something to eat – I could burn a meal as well as anyone! Over the meal Jimmy seemed demoralised (though not by my cooking) thinking about his wife Beebe, 'out and about again with that good-looking gigolo from the Savoy Hotel', a fair-haired guy with a handlebar moustache, who couldn't bear the sight of me – and I was not exactly in love with him either. (Many years later I discovered that he had been a pilot in the RFC during the war and afterwards found work first as a used car salesman then as a gigolo. His name was Bingham and it seems that in 1939 he obtained a commission in the RAF and finished as a high-ranking officer.) As for Beebe, I had fallen for her as only an 18-year-old youth can fall for a beautiful girl. I had spoken barely a dozen words to her but I still couldn't take my eyes off such a lovely 'dolly'! Jimmy named his solo record after her and before he went back to the States he gave me a wonderful gift – the original band parts of the tune, scored by Arthur Schutt, the pianist who had played during the late 1920s with Red Nichols and Paul Specht.

One afternoon Jimmy took me down to Bray to meet Ted Lewis and the members of his band, including that fiery trumpeter/cornettist Muggsy Spanier and trombonist George Brunis. He also introduced me to American bandleader Hal Kemp and one of his boys, Bunny Berigan. Kemp was playing then at the Café de Paris prior to an engagement at the Coliseum. Bunny Berigan was playing sweeter than in later years, but even then he was displaying that marvellous feeling for jazz on his trumpet.

Jimmy wanted me to go back to the US with him, but at the time there were many other things to be taken into consideration. My father was seriously ill in hospital, and that alone was enough to keep me from making the trip. After Jimmy had returned to the States I received a letter from the *Melody Maker* which said that they had heard a great deal about me and my work both at Grosvenor House and on records, 'including some very high praise from Jimmy Dorsey'.

Jimmy sent me the occasional Christmas card until we lost contact during the war years. Then early in 1947, singer Beryl Davis, writing to her father Harry Davis (leader of the Oscar Rabin band) from New York told of meeting Jimmy Dorsey at the Pennsylvania Hotel and that he wanted to be remembered to his old friends Joe Brannelly and Billy Amstell. Later that year, immediately prior to my joining Stanley Black's BBC Orchestra, Jimmy asked on a radio programme, called 'Atlantic Band Exchange', how Billy Amstell and Joe Brannelly were getting on. No one told me about this at the time: I eventually heard about it from trombonist Don Binney as we chatted one evening over a drink in the local.

7 'Whispering'

Early in January 1931 I auditioned for Roy Fox, the quietly spoken American bandleader with the smooth personality who, as a Musical Director for Decca, was responsible for their recording dance band. I was successful and joined the lineup which included trumpeter Arthur Niblo who was playing nights with me at Grosvenor House. The rest of the Decca House Band consisted of Max Goldberg (trumpet); Lew Davis (trombone); Ernest Ritte and Jim Easton (reeds); Ben Frankel (violin); Lew Stone (piano); Al Bowlly (guitar and vocals); Spike Hughes (string bass); and Bill Harty (drums). In four months we recorded 42 sides with Al Bowlly taking 39 vocals. Of the other three sides, Betty Bolton sang on one, the band on another, and there was just one instrumental – *Stardust*. We were strictly commercial!*

When Maurice Winnick heard that I was finishing at Grosvenor House, he at once offered me a job with his own band at the Piccadilly Hotel. I accepted, and I was pleased to find myself sitting beside Ben Frankel, the violinist with whom I had worked in the Decca House Band. We played many sessions together and became good friends: as a result, when he was asked to form an orchestra for film work, I was in it whenever I was free.

I had been with Maurice Winnick for only a few days when it was announced that a new night club, the Monseigneur, was to open right in the heart of Piccadilly and that Roy Fox was to provide the band. Maurice sportingly agreed to release me at the end of the week, at Roy's personal request.

On 27 May 1931 Roy Fox opened at the Monseigneur where rich red silks draped its dark blue walls and a large painting of Monseigneur hung near the cocktail bar. Our lineup showed a number of changes from the Decca House Band, from which only Lew Stone, Bill Harty, Al Bowlly and myself remained. Roy engaged Sid Buckman and Nat Gonella on trumpets and Joe Ferrie on trombone – the whole of Billy Cotton's brass section, and Bill never forgave him; indeed, when Roy returned to England in 1946 Bill opposed his working here. My brother Mick and Harry Berly (who also played viola and ocarina) completed the saxes and Don Stutely was on string bass.

Almost immediately the band was recognised as outstanding and we were scheduled for regular weekly broadcasts by the BBC. These went out on

---

*In those days Decca were operating from studios in Chelsea, where the artistes I backed included the former Danish boxing champion, Carl Brisson, who made his recording debut as a singer with *Cocktails for Two*, the trumpeter/bandleader Louis de Vries and singer Doris Hare who was also establishing herself as a revue artiste.

Wednesday nights, 10.30 to midnight, and we rapidly drew many thousands of listeners. I thought our brass section was good, likewise the reeds, especially the work of Harry Berly, but I thought the drumming was too loud and that the pianist could not be heard as an individual. Moreover, Al Bowlly was not one of my favourite guitarists. Roy was a nice guy to work for, although I certainly did not appreciate that 'whispering' cornet. One night the mute accidentally fell out and the ensuing sound was pretty awful! I loved the environment at the Monseigneur, and with the cabaret including Beatrice Lillie and Douglas Byng what more could one want? I was earning £15 a week plus the usual extra for recording and broadcasts and found life pretty good.

That is, until the day that Roy and his advisers in the band – Bill Harty, Lew Stone and Al Bowlly – decided to fire the second alto player – my brother Mick – and replace him with Ernest Ritte. I did not understand this. I had played with Ernest on many Decca House Band sessions and I had never heard him play an exposed solo, so I couldn't see where the improvement would be.

Playing commercial dance music six nights a week from 9pm until 2am for the society set who patronised the hotels and restaurants did tend to inhibit we musicians, especially those with strong jazz inclinations like myself. So, after finishing at the Monseigneur, it was my custom to make tracks for the London drinking clubs such as the Bag O'Nails in Kingly Street or the '43 Club in Gerrard Street, where I could 'let my hair down' by joining in the jam sessions that regularly developed there.

One day, while Mick was working out his notice, I received a telephone call asking if I would look in at Bert Ambrose's office and have a chat with Bert's secretary, Bill Williams. This I did, and it turned out that Ambrose's drummer, Max Bacon, having heard me 'giving out' at the '43 Club, had recommended me to his chief. Ambrose, leader of Britain's premier hotel, broadcasting and recording band and who had been resident at the May Fair Hotel for nearly four and a half years, was offering me a job in his reed section commencing on 1 September, following the usual summer break. Ambrose himself, a violinist/leader, was not a jazz player, but his orchestra had a reputation for being jazz-worthy, technically polished, renowned for its precision and most thoroughly proficient. I asked for a contract and was given one for six months. I suppose I was still a bit green: I stayed for nine years!

I left the Monseigneur on 11 August 1931 and went on holiday to Edinburgh with Mick, bandleader Lou Simmons, guitarist Harry Sherman and violinist Al Leslie, taking our instruments with us. On arrival we contacted Mr Bannister, the manager of the Marine Gardens, one of the largest ballrooms in Scotland, and were offered the use of his caravan for the whole of our vacation. This we gratefully accepted and did a few 'jam sessions' while we were there. We 'lived it up' a little, visiting the Havana Club in Princes Street, generally doing what we liked when we liked and only sleeping when we were too tired to stay awake! No one enjoyed themselves more than the extrovert Mick. I couldn't compete with this handsome chap whose personality was so attractive to everyone. He was also a great dancer

and held a cup for winning the Championship of London. I myself was an introvert –
and only a little over five feet tall, which is enough to give any chap a complex.

Having sewn a few wild oats it was now time to return to London and take up
my post with the famous Ambrose Orchestra, as second alto to Joe Crossman. I
took with me happy memories of Joe Ferrie, 'nice gent' Harry Berly and his superb
Lagonda in which he gave me the occasional lift – very different from my own 8hp
Singer Jnr – and Nat Gonella who had also been approached by Ambrose but
decided to stay on with Roy Fox on an improved contract.

8 Early Years at the May Fair Hotel

Entering the May Fair Hotel on the evening of 1 September 1931, I was instantly aware of more sumptuous surroundings. Sparkling bright, spotlessly clean and tastefully decorated, the whole place exhilarated me. The thick carpet gave one the impression of walking on air!

I made my way to the band room where Joe Jeannette, being the gentleman he is and always has been, welcomed me and showed me the locker that had been allocated to me. Max Goldberg, also making his début with the band that night, was the next to arrive. Max, who was a member of the HMV studio band under Ray Noble and had played with the Savoy Orpheans, gave me a friendly greeting in that heavy Canadian accent of his. As I unpacked my saxophone and clarinet and had a warming-up 'blow', several more of the boys arrived. Some nodded, others just said 'Hello, kid' and that's really all I was, a few days past my twentieth birthday. I found that instead of first night nerves I was full of curiosity about what was in store for me.

The room was almost full when Ambrose walked in on this first night back to work after the summer layoff. He looked Max and me over like an Arab restocking his harem, muttered, 'I'm sorry I changed the band' – and walked out again. Real encouragement, I thought. However, I soon discovered that 'Ammy', as the band referred to him, was always loathe to make changes and that his remark was not intended to be hurtful or discouraging. Although the others all adressed him as 'Bert', it was many months before I could bring myself to address him as anything except 'Mr Ambrose': that was the way I had been raised – to respect my elders. The band already had the reputation of being the premier broadcasting dance orchestra, so I knew I was with the best. The full lineup then was: Max Goldberg, Dennis Ratclife (trumpets); Ted Heath (trombone); Joe Crossman, Joe Jeannette, Billy Amstell (reeds); Bert Read (piano); Joe Brannelly (guitar); Dick Escott (bass); Max Bacon (drums); plus Ambrose himself playing the violin with that special soothing quality which made him so popular both at the May Fair and at the Embassy Club. The 'vocal refrains' were provided by Sam Browne of the pleasant tenor voice and perfect enunciation.

I wouldn't go so far as to say that I was rejected by the band during those first few weeks, rather that the boys were too taken up with their own pursuits to notice me. There was Joe Crossman, *Financial Times* under his arm when he wasn't playing tennis; Bert Read on the golf course, likewise Max Goldberg; two or three others out horse riding. Maybe I had a misguided sense of humour, but one evening a devilish mood came over me; I took a mustard pot from a table near the bandstand and coated Joe Crossman's baritone reed. He certainly played a 'hot' solo that night! Soon my antics were so popular that the only conversation I had with a fellow musician was with my inner self! It was Ted Heath who broke the ice when he told me not to fret; if the boys didn't like my ways I would soon fall in with theirs. Later, when I fell ill, I found out how really concerned and friendly they could be.

As soon as we began playing it was obvious that a feeling of intimacy existed between the band, Ambrose and the clientèle. Partly this was because the bandstand was raised no more than six inches above the dance floor. We provided music from 9.30pm until 2am six nights a week, playing all the popular tunes of the day, including the latest Broadway 'show stoppers'. In the cabaret was a troupe of lovely dancing girls trained by Buddy Bradley, a true perfectionist among dance directors. Two of the girls in particular I remember – Moira (who later married Ted Heath) amd Googie Withers who of course went on to a distinguished acting career. These two were friends and I thought Googie was really something although I was too shy to speak to her! Comedian Ted Ray was also part of the cabaret, cracking his favourite joke – 'She asked me back to her flat for a whisky and sofa. I didn't drink but I went!'

On some nights during the week, towards 2am when most of the patrons had left the restaurant, some of the special arrangements which were to be featured on the Saturday night broadcasts were introduced, in a way using the time to rehearse them. I really came alive with these numbers which were important to me. They were far more interesting than the routine three choruses of the standard numbers – three choruses and no exposed solos.* Joe Brannelly was partly responsible for the band's keenness and enthusiasm; being an American, he was able to secure arrangements from the States, especially those of Jimmy Dorsey, in exchange for some of Ambrose's manuscripts. Joe came to England in 1924; he had been asked by the Savoy Hotel Entertainments Manager to bring over Rudy Vallee to join the Havana Band. With them came the modest 21-year-old piano player Carroll Gibbons. All three had been in college together. Rudy's ambition was to be Mayor of New York City, but he had eventually to settle for being the first crooner/bandleader, a radio and recording star with another career in pictures. He invited Joe and myself to spend our summer holiday in 1933 in the States, using his apartment as our base. Joe was free to go but I had the bad luck to develop septic tonsils, so instead of Rudy's apartment my holiday base was a hospital having them removed. Carroll Gibbons, because of his American drawl, was asked to play a part in the BBC production of John Steinbeck's *Of Mice and Men*; but he had a stammer and was not at all at ease in front of a microphone. However, someone had the bright idea of having Carroll speak his lines seated at the piano, and so the problem was solved.

I made the first of many Saturday night broadcasts with Ambrose from the May

*There were complaints of course: the customers complained that it was too loud; the management complained; when 'Ammy' came back he told us to stop it, but as soon as he had gone we went back to the 'music', the arrangements.

Fair on 12 September (1931). For these weekly broadcasts an addition to our personnel was that most popular singer Elsie Carlisle, who also had a great gift for comedy. When she duetted with Sam Browne they made a fine team, still remembered by many with enormous affection.

Ambrose was recording for HMV when I joined his band, and when the May Fair nights approached 2am I found that I was a wee bit tired but looking forward to being in the studio for recording sessions just eight hours later. I well remember the second session on 16 September. This included Kalmar and Ruby's *Nevertheless* on which, following the Sam Browne vocal there was an alto solo by – ME! Joe Crossman didn't speak to me for about two weeks afterwards because no one, I discovered, had ever before played an alto solo in his presence. Bert Read, who had made the arrangement, appeared most uncomfortable! However, I think that Joe did get round to liking me on account of the way I would glide around with him as second alto . . . no one could follow him the way I did and I reckon he appreciated it. This went on until Joe left to join Lew Stone at the Monseigneur late in October 1932. He was replaced by the great American reed player Danny Polo in his second spell with the band, for he had played with Ambrose at the May Fair for 18 months in 1929 and 1930. When Joe Crossman arrived at the Bag O'Nails where, as I have said, many musicians went for a 'blow' after work, whoever was playing clarinet packed up, including me. The one exception was Danny Polo – then Joe would quit the club!

It was during these autumn recording sessions that Joe Jeannette was so kind and helpful as I changed from Simple system to Boehm clarinet. He wrote out little exercises for me and demonstrated the Boehm fingering. He also instilled into me the necessity of wearing a clean collar every night and a clean shirt every other night and telling me to show at least half an inch of shirt cuff beyond my coat sleeve. Also, he stipulated for my benefit that bow ties had to come from Scotts in Piccadilly. His shoes were handmade: I didn't go quite that far, but mine were still of good quality. Sam Browne volunteered to take me to his tailor, Wainer, who gave me extra care: the cost of a dinner suit with the best quality facing was £10 in 1931. My initial salary of £16 a week had soon risen to £20 plus £4 for a recording session and £3 for a broadcast. With more than two million unemployed I was indeed one of the lucky ones. In October 1931 we played the London Palladium with the band augmented to 18 pieces.

The hotel swing doors with the portholes were for the staff. Through these the waiters rushed in and out all night. One evening in 1932 I noticed a fair-haired fellow whose eyes were popping out of his head as he watched the waiters hurrying through the doors laden with trays. I thought he was probably anticipating one of them making the mistake of going through the IN door when he should have taken the OUT, no doubt causing an almighty clash of trays! He was still there when it was time for our interval. Joe Brannelly sensed that he was a fellow American and introduced himself – 'Hello, man, my name's Joe.' Came back the reply – 'Howdy; my name's Hoagy.' 'How d'you do, Hoagy?' I said. 'My name's Billy . . .' And that is how I met the great Hoagland Carmichael. Having heard so much about

31

Ambrose in the States he had decided to see and hear for himself. Ambrose was the first British band to play a regular 30-minute radio programme in the US, and early in 1931 they had recorded Hoagy's *Stardust*. The arrangement was by Bert Read with a beautiful verse played by Joe Crossman. Later that night Hoagy sat in the lounge with Ambrose and the American-born band leader Howard Jacobs. Hoagy was an extremely quiet guy who left most of the talking to the other two. Years later, when I deputised at the London Casino for the Hoagy spot in the programme, I mentioned our meeting at the May Fair and he remembered it well. We met again later still when I was with Stanley Black's BBC Orchestra, and once more he had not forgotten me. A sleepy looking fellow he may have been; but he was a good listener with a wonderful memory.

That much-respected Bostonian Howard Jacobs, of the good looks and immaculate dress, was bandleader at the nearby Berkeley Hotel and would often slip into the May Fair for a chat with 'Ammy' during interval time. Whenever I was on my way to the Coventry Street Corner House I would never fail to stop by the Berkeley and listen from the street to Howard Jacobs' band, and especially to the tenor player, Johnny Helfer, a lovely instrumentalist and very presentable. I never did speak to either of them apart from saying 'good evening' to Howard Jacobs as I passed him and Ambrose on my way to the bandstand. I was still a shy sort of guy!

Whenever I gave Max Bacon a lift in my little car to the Corner House after work, the Singer always became lopsided, to the amusement of my other passenger, Sam Browne. Max, of course, weighed more than 20 stone.

As we entered the Corner House one night I came face to face with Jack Shields, the alto player I had replaced in the Ambrose Orchestra. My hand went out to him, but he completely ignored me.

Music was also playing an important rôle at the Dorchester Hotel in Park Lane, where the Blue Lyres, an Ambrose unit, had succeeded the Melville Gideon band and was making quite an impact under the leadership of saxophonist Arthur Lally. Arthur's personal success, however, was halted by illness, and one night when he was too ill to broadcast, Ambrose rushed me over in his Bentley as replacement. It was a bitterly cold night and I caught a chill which developed into pneumonia (shades of Bix Beiderbecke!). It was, in fact, a very near thing for me as the recovery rate from pneumonia all those years ago was nowhere near as high as it is now.

Recuperating in Torquay, I became interested in the flute which I studied for some three years before giving it up as I thought it was interfering with my work on clarinet and saxophone.

Once back in harness with Ambrose, I found that the band was still in great demand at the HMV studios where during my first 11 months 120 titles were recorded – the equivalent of ten LPs! The majority of our arrangements were written by Sid Phillips and Bert Read plus some by Ronnie Munro. For recording purposes the orchestra was augmented by three violins – Ernie Lewis, Teddy Sinclair and Peter Rush – and by Harry Owen on trumpet. Elsie Carlisle and Sam Browne provided nearly all the vocals, although there were a few by Ella Logan who duetted with Sam on *I Don't Know Why* for her last recording with Ambrose prior to sailing for America to further her career on radio, stage and in films. Ella was an aunt of those well-known Scottish entertainers Annie Ross and Jimmy Logan.

Throughout my first years with Ambrose at the May Fair, I also played on a good many recordings with Spike Hughes's orchestra, winning myself some excellent reviews in *Melody Maker*. There was moreover a treat in store – Ambrose and the band were booked into Monte Carlo for four weeks that summer and I would have my twenty-first birthday there. Early in 1932 Don Stuteley had replaced Dick Escott on string bass; otherwise there were no other changes to the personnel between my arrival and our departure for Monte Carlo. Ambrose did indeed like as little change as possible in his band.

9 Monte Carlo and the May Fair Again

Our first adventure in Monte Carlo began at the Customs where the officer in charge was pondering whether or not to make us all strip – until he caught Max Bacon twitching an eye. Max's nervous trick of winking was well known to his friends but evidently the *douanier* was not among them. One twitch from Max was enough and the officer ordered a thorough search of his luggage. Out shot shoes, shirts, studs, socks, ties and three pairs of woollen 'combs' – ideal for a Mediterranean summer! I think the fellow must have held the Scout's badge for thoroughness, for another wink from Max and he was doing an Xavier Cugat act with the side drums. Hearing the snares vibrate and thinking he had uncovered a cachet of heroin, he was quietened only when Max pulled the thing apart to prove his point that Customs officials are not always right.

We were staying at the exclusive Metropole Villas, adjacent to the Metropole Hotel. The chef had prepared a meal of roast beef and Yorkshire pudding to make us feel at home, and although we all appreciated the gesture, for myself I would have been happy with a salt-beef sandwich! Joe Crossman, a vegetarian, asked for a salad, which came up without delay. This was my first visit to Monte Carlo and I was suitably impressed, in contrast with the blasé I've-seen-everything-and-the-postcards-too attitude of some members of the band.

'Ammy' was engaged to play at the New Beach Casino, playground of the 'idle rich', where one could feel the close proximity of the tranquil sea. The dancing took place upstairs in what was known as the 'Night Club', which had a glass dance floor with multi-coloured lights underneath and produced a remarkable effect. The cabaret dancers were the well-known Bal Tabarin Girls, and with an eye to keeping the gamblers in the right frame of mind, no less than four bands were engaged. In this sub-tropical climate, music for outdoor dancing was provided by the famous American Orchestra led by Lud Gluskin, the equally famous Latin–American band of Don Aspiazu, a very entertaining French Tango band – and Ambrose. It was a fascinating experience for me to meet Lud Gluskin and some of his boys, including Danny Polo whose superlative clarinet playing impressed everyone. Then there was Gene Prendergast, one-time tenor player with the Casa Loma Orchestra; also the late Emile Christian who had one time played trumpet in New Orleans before switching to trombone when he came to England with the Original Dixieland Jazz Band after the Great War. Emile was a nice guy; he went to the Continent after England and I was saddened when I heard later that he had died.

The Metropole Villas were quite a distance from the New Beach Casino swimming pool. The boys in the band were so used to the best things in life that we would hail the nearest buggie. In would get Sam Browne, Ted Heath, Bert Read the 'lumberer', and myself, the odd man out being Max Goldberg who sat up front with the driver, explaining where to take us in his best heavy Canadian French accent. As we took the same route as the Monte Carlo Rally round the bend at the Terminus Hotel and slowed down, Bert Read signalled us to get out, which we did, the idea being that the last man out pays! Max Goldberg was careful not to sit up with the driver next time . . .

One night when our band had completed a spell and the French band had taken over, I wandered along to the end of the terrace, where the Don Aspiazu band was also taking a break, to have a chat with Chico, the bongo player – a lad of about my own age with whom I had been rowing a couple of times in the harbour. The boys were sitting in a circle passing round what appeared to me to be a cigarette. Later Chico explained that it was actually a 'weed', or 'joint'. One would never have suspected that the boys were 'high' because they were always such a happy bunch anyway. This was all new to me . . . but the lad from the East End of London was learning fast!

After our night's work at the Casino had finished, we used to frequent one of the all-night cafés in the resort for a few drinks and a chat. Some of the girls we met there were 'on the game'! It so happened that we were in the café on my twenty-first birthday; Bert Read, the 'lumberer' (joker), started to get busy. He guessed which of the girls I fancied . . . but she, being new to the business, was as hesitant as I was, so neither of us had the nerve to make a pass. Bert, having found out how much 'it' cost, came to me for the money, which I promptly handed over. That was the last I saw of him that night: I hope he had a 'good time' at my expense!

One of the outstanding artistes at the Casino was Marion Harris. This attractive young singer with the silky voice would perform most of her act sitting on the piano top, which was pretty 'way out' in those days. She stunned us with her version of *Singing the Blues*, her own lyrics to the Frankie Trumbauer/Bix Beiderbecke choruses, delivered in a truly rhythmic style. She was a great favourite and was often in the company of Edward, Prince of Wales, and his brother Prince George – and Ambrose. The two princes were frequent visitors to the night club, dancing away unrecognised by the patrons. The little village up in the hills at Mont Agel boasted an exclusive golf club where the Prince of Wales and Ambrose would play a few rounds together. 'Ammy' was the better golfer, but he would sometimes joke that the Prince had won a couple of bob from him!

Only one bandleader could have recorded in Monte Carlo at that time – Ambrose. He arranged for all the technicians and equipment to be transported from the HMV studios in London, and on 22 August we recorded six titles, all with vocals by Sam Browne, in the unused ground floor of the Metropole Hotel. Three numbers I remember were, *Happy Go Lucky You (And Broken Hearted Me)*, *Masquerade*, and *Nothing But A Lie*. I also recollect that the labels stated that the recordings were made in Monte Carlo.

We returned home early in September to resume our residency at the May Fair Hotel, again broadcasting from there every Saturday night. When Joe Crossman moved over to Lew Stone's band, Ambrose invited Danny Polo to join us. As I filled in on first alto and clarinet pending his arrival, I thought how satisfying it was going to be to have such a swell American musician in the band.* When he came, 'Ammy' got stuck on one of his bright ideas. Looking at Joe Jeannette and me one evening, he suggested we changed places there and then. Not being the types to argue with the boss, we got to work on each other's saxes. That was how things were done in the Ambrose band! Later we became organised on the deal and I traded my baritone for Joe's tenor; but that initial rapid change was my first day on tenor.

It was certainly an experience sitting alongside Danny listening to his stories of playing with the legendary Bix Beiderbecke around the Chicago night spots and even in the whorehouses, and of the time when he was in the Ben Pollack band. He told me that when Pollack's outfit packed up at 2am, a trio took over for the late-nighters. It comprised a pianist, a drummer and a young lad of some sixteen years, none other than the great Benny Goodman! Danny it was who introduced me to my first smoke of 'pot' when he gave me a marijuana cigarette in the boiler room of the May Fair Hotel one New Year's Eve. There was no doubt that it gave me a 'lift': I was awake until around 6am! I tried it again two or three times, but it exhilarated me so much that I got scared and gave it up.

By the end of 1932 I thought the band was in pretty good shape. All the boys were showing more and more interest in the US jazz scene, via records and short wave radio. Joe Brannelly was continuing to bring in some of the more modern arrangements by such as the Casa Loma band, the Dorseys and Duke Ellington which we would bring out for an airing in the small hours despite the usual complaints and 'Ammy's' admonishing forefinger.

I was doing some arrangements myself at this time – *Pink Elephants* (for which Francis, Day and Hunter sent me £5), *If I Let You Get Away with it Now*, *It Don't Mean a Thing* (Lawrence Wright paid me six guineas for that), *That's A-Plenty*; and I rescored *Swanee*, on which Nat Gonella played a beautiful introduction (that Oriole record is now a collector's item). All these were broadcast by Ambrose; indeed, one Saturday night broadcast contained eight of my arrangements.

In 1933 Ambrose was recognised as the leader of Europe's finest dance band, playing to capacity audiences at the May Fair. Early in that year he signed a contract for his band to appear exclusively on the Brunswick label, and we soon proved that we could hold our own with a host of American units in that catalogue,

*In those days a number of foreign musicians, mostly Americans, could be found in British dance bands. It was not until 1935 that the Musicians' Union persuaded the Ministry of Labour to impose that untenable ban which denied (with a few exceptions) work permits to overseas musicians. The ban lasted for some twenty years until the MU agreed reciprocal arrangements with the American Federation of Musicians. Danny Polo first arrived in this country early in 1929 direct from the Jean Goldkette Orchestra and, apart from his first engagement with Ambrose, had been greatly in demand for recording sessions over here, for he was a jazz-orientated player, featuring in Bert Firman's Rhythmic Eight on the Zonophone label and with Philip Lewis' Rhythm Maniacs and Spike Hughes's Dance Band for Decca.

from Guy Lombardo to Duke Ellington. By the end of July we had recorded a further 80 titles. The only change in the personnel that I can recall was Harry Hayes for Harry Hines on recording sessions.

During that summer break Max Goldberg invited me to join him on a touring holiday in his new Austin Twelve/Six saloon. It seemed pretty attractive, but . . . we motored down to Falmouth arriving there tired out . . . set off early next morning for Lands End, and so on . . . rushing around and getting nowhere fast. One night we stayed at a hotel in Exeter where Maxie thought a little physical exercise would do him good. The evening was drawing in as he stripped off in front of the window of our room. Suddenly we heard giggling but could not make out where it was coming from – until we realised that our room was at the rear of the building facing the staff quarters. It was no wonder we heard the girls giggling, with Max being so well endowed! He was a very fit guy and always enjoyed his golf no matter what the weather was like. He once took me out to practise approach shots with a number five iron out of bunkers. That was OK by me, but he had me at it for at least four hours. When we returned to London I needed another holiday.

I have many amusing memories of the May Fair Hotel in 1933 – not least of one Saturday night following the close of a broadcast. As we resumed playing for the patrons, Ted Heath, who had been blowing away all through without wearing his dentures (as usual), pulled a handkerchief out of his top pocket to mop his brow and was dismayed to see (and hear) the false teeth bounce across the dance floor!

A final memory of that year at the May Fair, and one I am sure I shall always retain, is of Duke Ellington on his first visit to England dining downstairs at the express invitation of the Prince of Wales. The long table accommodated the whole Ellington band with Duke at one end and the Prince, who was a great jazz lover, at the other, with Ambrose, who the Prince had insisted be included, next to him. We of the Ambrose Orchestra watched from close by, drinking in the whole scene. Indeed, the Prince and Ambrose were on terms of friendship to the extent that 'Ammy's flat was at the Prince's disposal at all times. He was able to avail himself of this facility whenever he could manage to slip away from the bodyguards Queen Mary had appointed to watch over him.

I see from my diary that I was also active that year recording for Joe Brannelly, Sam Browne, Tommy Kinsman and Johnny Raitz, besides doing film work for Bert Read's Cartoon and Elsie Carlisle's appearance in the picture *Radio Parade*, plus a radio date or two for Harry Bidgood. Busy life!

Earlier in the year Ambrose had made an addition to the orchestra for a period of four or five months – to give some extra flavour to the Latin–American numbers. This was none other than my old friend Chico, the bongo player from the Don Aspiazu band we had played alongside in Monte Carlo the previous year.

10 'Embassy Stomp'

After six and a half years at the May Fair Hotel, Ambrose decided to return to the scene of his first success in this country in the early 1920s. We opened at the fashionable Embassy Club in Bond Street on 26 September 1933.

On that first night I was thrilled to see my 'film hero' Douglas Fairbanks Snr sitting at a table very near the bandstand and right in front of me. He was accompanied by Lady Sylvia Ashley, and other first-nighters included the Queen of Spain and her two daughters, the Marks and Spencer families, the American golfer Charles Sweeny, the Woolworth heiress Barbara Hutton of the very pale complexion, and that lovely old gentleman the Duke of Wellington who always made a point of shaking Ambrose by the hand. The place was so packed that the dance floor was almost non-existent.

'Ammy' was without doubt the darling of the society set. It was the late Maurice Burman (drummer with the bands of Roy Fox and Geraldo) who described him so aptly: 'Like most outstanding people Ambrose is very "human" and naturally modest. He has a rare mixture of dignity and buffoonery; he is a shrewd, subtle and sophisticated man, independent of spirit, proud yet incapable of being snobbish, talking to waiters as he did to princes, and princes as he did to waiters, treating everybody as he found them.'

Musically I felt the band was reaching its peak during the Embassy Club period. Our recordings of *Hors D'Oeuvres* and *Embassy Stomp* (both arranged by Bert Barnes; the second also composed by him), and the Sid Phillips numbers *B'Wanga* and *Streamline Strut*, plus *Dodging a Divorcée* and *Copenhagen* were only a foretaste of things to come. The band had been augmented by Sid on baritone sax and clarinet, and by Lew Davis and Tony Thorpe making up the famous trombone trio with Ted Heath. After a while Dick Escott returned on string bass; Bert Barnes replaced Bert Read (who moved over to Henry Hall at the BBC) early in 1935 and Harry Owen was on second trumpet, with Elsie Carlisle and the dependable Sam Browne looking after the vocals. I was taking all the tenor sax solos, Danny Polo the clarinet solos, with Bert Barnes, Max Goldberg and Lew Davis as the other leading soloists. Ambrose browbeat at least one arrangement out of every member of the band, and this gave some of the boys migraine! Max Goldberg, a bright boy at the game, produced an ear-worthy effort – *Piccaninny* I believe it was – but his manuscript looked like a Greek poem and Joe Jeannette suggested that Max must have written it with his feet!

Between October 1933 and early June 1934 we recorded 74 titles for the Brunswick label – the equivalent of six or seven full LPs. I had been otherwise busy again in 1934, doing quite a few dates at Decca for Elsie Carlisle and one at HMV for Marek Weber's only session in this country. This well-known German bandleader had built up quite a reputation playing jazz back in the 1920s. I also did some work for Ronnie Munro at the Elstree Film Studios.

It was a great treat one night in early March, after I had finished at the Embassy Club, to go along to the Astoria to hear the American showman/bandleader Cab Calloway and his unit on their first appearance in this country. I was delighted when he included *Minnie the Moocher*, the number he had made so much his own.

Late in July, the Embassy Club having given their permission, Ambrose and his orchestra travelled to Biarritz, rooming at the Hôtel Angleterre until 21 September. During our stay we learned that 'Ammy' had lost £28,000 in one night at the Casino tables! He was a generous man, as gamblers often are, always treating his musicians to a night out or a meal on the train. One teatime on a train I was feeling a bit embarrassed as usual and plucked up my courage to ask him: 'Bert, let me pay for the tea.' He looked at me in a paternal sort of way, and said, 'Do you really want to pay, Billy?' 'Yes,' I replied. 'Well then,' said 'Ammy', 'I'll tell you what I'll do. Since you're such a nice boy I'll let you pay next time.' Of course that next time never came. Bert would never dream of allowing any of his men to pay for anything. He wanted the very best for his musicians – all the time – including the finest accommodation and we always stayed at the quality hotels.

It was in Biarritz that I met André Dessary; he was 23 years old, like myself, and already Professor of Physical Culture. His father was the local postmaster and from the telegrams passing between London and Biarritz these two fans of the Ambrose band knew exactly when we would be arriving. André persuaded me to visit his gymnasium three times a week for a workout with weights, etc and a full strength, long distance hosing down which almost took my breath away. This treatment did me a power of good: I took the punishment for nearly eight weeks, expanding my narrow chest by four and a half inches! Accompanying me to the gym was Eddie Foy, alto sax player in the famous Ray Ventura orchestra, which was playing opposite us for the season. Eddie tried his best to get me to join Ray Ventura, who did in fact make me a very fair offer, but I was too happy playing alongside the likes of Danny Polo and Max Goldberg. Had I accepted I would in the course of time have played to André Dessary's singing, for he was already fancying himself as a vocalist when I met him and later became featured singer with the Ventura band. He never neglected, though, to have the whole band doing physical training on the beach whenever they played a summer season on the coast! Eventually André branched out as a solo singer-cum-entertainer on radio and in films, and became a household name on the Continent. Some years ago, jazz trombonist Chris Barber telephoned me from Paris and passed on best wishes from André – they had been on the same radio programmes together that day. The last I heard of Eddie Foy was that during the war years he had been a member of the French Resistance.

While in Biarritz we were told that Edward, Prince of Wales, had given his bodyguards the slip and dived into the sea to rescue a young lad who had got into difficulties in the treacherous currents. So as to protect the bodyguards from the wrath of Buckingham Palace, the story was kept out of the newspapers.

The large café opposite the Hôtel Angleterre was a rendezvous for British holidaymakers as well as for the boys in the band. There was a lady cashier who had a snappy little dog that was given to barking and growling, especially at Max Bacon. With the cashier so frequently calling '*Ici, ici*' Max christened the little animal 'Issy', althouth I think only the boys in the band saw the joke. Max (of all people!) taught Benito, the local semi-pro drummer, a few words of English – the usual coarse and crude phrases one comes to expect in such circumstances – with the result that poor Benito's use of certain words in the crowded café made most of the British customers shudder!

We returned to the Embassy Club in late September and from mid-October resumed recording for Decca. By the following August we had put about 140 more titles on wax. The augmented orchestra not only showed an unexcelled precision and technical ability on the instrumental numbers I have already mentioned, but no less on the ballads like *I Get a Kick out of You, Dinner at Eight* and *The Show is Over*, all with fine vocals by Sam Browne. By the mid-1930s the band had a big following in the United States too and one night I heard over short wave radio Jimmy Dorsey announce . . . 'and now the Ambrose arrangement of *Hors D'Oeuvres.*' Evidently we had something to offer the Americans!

Early in 1935 Ambrose decided not to allow any substantial contingent of his star players to record for any other bandleader. Several of the boys had been identified playing for George Scott-Wood on the exciting 'Six Swingers' recordings for Regal Zonophone. Happily, however, 'Ammy's' decision did not deprive the fans of this type of music, for he arranged with Decca to supply an eight-piece lineup from within the orchestra – a kind of anticipation of the 'band within a band' concept followed by many of the big white American bands during the 'Swing' era (the Benny Goodman small groups; Tommy Dorsey's Clambake Seven; Artie Shaw's Gramercy Five; and others) – to make swing recordings under the name 'The Embassy Eight'. The original group comprised Max Goldberg, Lew Davis, Danny Polo, Bert Barnes, Joe Brannelly, Dick Ball, Max Bacon and myself. We kicked off with four titles from the 1920s – *He's a Rag Picker, Hitchy Koo, Where the Black Eyed Susan's Grow, Back Home in Tennessee* – played in a really 'hot' style. The *Melody Maker* reported that Decca were on to a winner.

The highlight of 1935 was our radio augmented orchestra's* 'Grand Concert in Rhythm' on 30 June at the Royal Opera House, Covent Garden – the first and only time a big dance band appeared in concert there. Such a unique event surely merits a place in the annals of 'live' performances of 'rhythmic' music. Among an audience of 2000 there were many who had come from all over Europe to hear this two and a half hour concert sponsored by the *Melody Maker*.

Another triumph for Ambrose that year concerns the American singer Connie (or Connee) Boswell of the famous Boswell Sisters close harmony singing trio. Connie, who had suffered a disabling attack of polio in childhood and made all her

*See Appendix.

public appearances in a wheelchair, had never sung solo with a big dance band before; but 'Ammy' with his exceptional powers of persuasion managed to get her to do just that. On 19 July she recorded four titles with the band, including *I'll Never Say Never Again Again* and *Things Might Have been so Different*, and shortly afterwards she was persuaded to sing solo with the band on a Saturday night broadcast from the BBC studios, where the microphones were hung from the roof. She was wheeled into the studio and two of the staff lifted her very gently onto a back-support stool for her to sing *I'll Never Say Never* into the mike.

Frequent visitors to the Embassy Club included the Prince of Wales, escorting Mrs Wallis Simpson, and Prince George with Princess Marina. The heir apparent never failed to give Bert Ambrose a nod, and a smile to the band, as he and his party took their usual seats to the left of the bandstand. Joe Brannelly used to take some of the latest Broadway show music to the Prince of Wales; and on one occasion he took a pair of drumsticks: the Prince fancied himself as a jazz drummer!

One Thursday night at the Embassy – a late drinks night – Princess Marina and Prince George arrived fresh from their honeymoon and, with a small party, went to their usual places in the top left-hand corner. As we played all the great tunes of Cole Porter, Jerome Kern, Irving Berlin, etc several times a night we knew most of them from memory, so we were able to look over all the diners, noting this and that.

On this particular Thursday night Joe Jeannette nudged me and said: 'Watch this.' Just then Gualdi, the Italian manager, passed on his way from the kitchens. 'Hey, Gualdi!' said Joe, 'Miss Carroll [Madeleine Carroll the actress who was sitting close by with the Hon Ivor Guest] 'is wearing the same dress as the Princess!' A stream of Italian came from Gualdi who with hands clasped behind his back walked up the room bowing right and left (there was no room to dance) and then came back to Miss Carroll and Ivor Guest. After he had spoken to them in low tones they got up and left through the kitchens, into the staff passage and out into Piccadilly. The same thing happened on another occasion to Miss Tilly Marks, sister of Lord Simon Marks, and the famous actress Gladys Cooper. They caught sight of each other at exactly the same time, and had the same thought. Then both rose and went to the exit door where they compared notes. I pitied their dress designers!

Something always seemed to happen on a Thursday night. I remember Joe nudging me once – and I looked up and saw, right in front of me, Prince Aly Khan stroking the eyebrows of a blonde with his tongue. There was such a crush on the dance floor that they couldn't move for nearly a minute, by which time the girl was on the point of swooning!

I daresay that none of this escaped the attention of Colonel Edgerton, the Club Secretary, without whose permission no one could acquire membership. This tall, elegant, slim dark-haired man with a military moustache was a well known personality around the West End. Today I can still visualise his upright figure in Bond Street on his way to the Club in his high wing collar and with his immaculate tails flying in the breeze. A character from bygone days who, incidentally, held Ambrose in very high esteem.

Our 12-piece band (with 'Ammy' on violin) continued playing for the society set at the Embassy until late July 1935. It had become 'the rage of Mayfair for its refined dance music', as one critic put it. However, it was now time for Ambrose and his Orchestra to go 'on the road' and let the great British public see and hear us around the country.

11   On the Road

Before leaving London we played for two weeks from 29 July at the Palladium, where we were overwhelmed by our rapturous receptions. The ensuing tour took us to venues in many cities and towns, including the Glasgow and Edinburgh Empires, the Marine Gardens Edinburgh, the Piccadilly Club in Glasgow, the Grafton Rooms in Liverpool, Southport, and the Tower Ballroom, Blackpool.

It was at a Sunday (11 August 1935) concert in Blackpool – there must have been about five or six thousand people present – that the vivacious and curvacious American 'Blonde Bombshell' Evelyn Dall made her début. She was a lovely, very attractive girl, with a beautiful face and fair hair and a lovely figure. When she ran on her boobs bounced up and down and wrong notes kept coming from the band. Ambrose couldn't make out what was going on and where the wrong notes were coming from. She must have been one of the first females to appear on stage without a bra. The boys in the band were taking their eyes off their music and looking at her – so out came the wrong notes and the more puzzled did 'Ammy' become! He had brought her over from the States as a replacement for Elsie Carlisle who had gone off on tour with Sam Browne. He could not have made a better choice, for audiences everywhere warmed to her breezy personality and simply loved her whenever she appeared.

Ambrose introduced Evelyn with *South American Joe*, and at the end of it he thought a 16-inch gun had gone off! We had never heard such applause. Evelyn soon became a big hit all over the country, for she not only broadcast and made films and recordings but became one of the first television stars, appearing nearly every day in one programme or another.

Alas, the war came and she returned to the States where she married and settled down to a happy life and was heard and seen no more.

For these tours the percussion was very demanding, so 'Ammy' hired a second drummer for them. This was George Elrick, the Scottish drummer/vocalist who later joined Henry Hall and the BBC Dance Orchestra and later still became a popular radio disc jockey.

There was another memorable incident at the Tower Ballroom, Blackpool. We opened the second half of the programme with *Rhapsody in Blue*. Danny Polo played the clarinet introduction and then the piano should have followed in. But there was a silence: we looked round and there was Bert Barnes, our pianist, slumped! He'd had too much to drink. Bert was always a heavy drinker, but this time he had gone one too far and too many. Quick as a flash 'Ammy' snapped out:

'Into the next number.' It all went well enough then; but there was blue murder when we came off the stand!

There came a time later when Bert (Barnes) visited his doctor for some tests, and when we enquired about the result, Bert quipped with a doleful smile: 'He's discovered blood in my alcohol stream!'

Returning to London we played the Holborn Empire early in November with five brass, four saxes and four rhythm. Our personnel showed little change, with the familiar names all in place – Max Goldberg, Harry Owen (t); Lew Davis, Ted Heath, Tony Thorpe (tb); Danny Polo, Joe Jeannette, Billy Amstell, Sid Phillips (reeds); Bert Barnes (p); Joe Brannelly (g); Dick Ball (b); Max Bacon (d); Evelyn Dall (vcl).

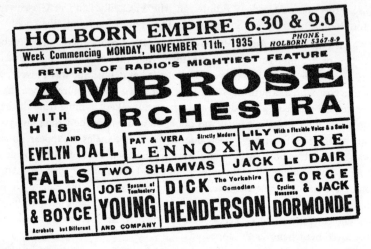

When we appeared again at the Holborn Empire the following March, the billing read: **Ambrose's Orchestra Including Max Bacon and Personally Conducted By The Blonde Bombshell Evelyn Dall**. 'Ammy' was taking a break.

A bombshell of another sort exploded on 5 June 1936 when the national evening newspaper *The Star* reported that Ambrose had been offered £600 a week to tour the USA for a few months as a dance band conductor, taking with him his crooner, his drummer, and his music arrangers. The *Daily Express* reported: 'I [Ambrose] don't want to go, but English audiences have finally forced me . . . they do not want good music. They don't seem to understand it. All they want from a bandleader is clowning and I can't clown . . .'

'Ammy' was most indignant when he read that. He said he had been grossly misquoted and 'never slept a wink last night . . . the British public couldn't have been sweeter to me . . . I'm going to America for three months . . . to say I am dissolving the band! . . . the band I have taken years to assemble! It is disgraceful and wicked . . . I have issued a writ against the *Express* . . . Tonight from the stage of the Liverpool Empire I will have to make a statement . . . must let the public know they haven't driven me out . . . they do understand good music.'

Happily the whole matter subsided; we continued our tour and 'Ammy's' 'American connection' never materialised.

In July 1936 we played a week in Plymouth where a new and impressive swimming pool had just been opened, complete with a lifeguard, powerfully built and standing well over six feet. One afternoon our band-boy, Reg Anscombe, was at the side of the pool with some of the band, admiring an extremely attractive girl in a white swim suit. Reg, himself a good looking lad with black wavy hair, 'toothbrush' moustache and athletic figure, rather fancied his chances with this eye-catching young lady and turning to the lifeguard remarked, 'I could do her a bit of good'; whereupon the lifeguard glared hard at him and after a slight pause retorted: 'That is my wife!' Poor Reggie shrunk.

Although we spent so much time touring up and down the country, we managed to visit the Decca studios in London to wax another 80 titles between September 1935 and the middle of the following August. One of our outstanding instrumentals of this time was Sid Phillips's *Night Ride*. By June 1936 there had been a complete change over in the brass section, with Clinton Ffrench and Teddy Foster on

trumpets and Eric Breeze and Don MaCaffer alongside Lew Davis on trombones. Teddy Foster originally played trombone but switched to trumpet. On tour Ambrose would feature him singing *Old Man Mose Kicked the Bucket* à la Louis Armstrong.

Max Bacon, besides being a top class drummer was also no mean Jewish comic, very popular with audiences with his 'fractured' English (among other peculiarities was that he could never manage the letter 'v' which invariably came out as 'w', so that a word like 'seven' always sounded as 'sewen'). They all knew his *William T'hell* and *Little Red Hooding Ride* ('whoever's slipper this is can be my missis') routines, plus his recordings of *Cohen the Crooner*, *Knock, Knock, Who's There?*, *Shut the Door (They're Coming Through the Window)* and *When Gimble Hits the Cymbal* which featured his solid drumming, the famous line 'Come on Sammy

Cohen, let's hear you play that saxophoen' sung by Sam and featuring Ambrose, for the only time on record, speaking the introduction.

When singer Jack Cooper joined the band Max used him on stage as his 'straight' man. Cooper's first name was really 'Bert', but as we already had Bert Barnes as well as our leader being another 'Bert', Ambrose insisted that he be known as 'Jack' – to roars of laughter from the band, which prompted Bert Ambrose to utter his familiar admonition, 'Don't fuss, fellows, don't fuss!' So Jack Cooper it was; but to Max Bacon in his stage act he was always 'Jimmy'.

Max worked with Ambrose nearly all his drumming life. He knew perhaps more than most 'Ammy's' constant demand for musical perfection. Max believed that if you were not feeling so good or even were really ill it meant nothing to Bert – death was the only excuse! Despite his fine drumming, never obtrusive but played with real 'lift' plus his deft technique on the cymbal, Max came in for his share of Bert's criticism. Many times he handed in his notice because of 'Ammy's' strict discipline. Once when he had an extremely painful boil on his neck and could hardly move, let alone play, Ambrose kept nagging at him. At the end of the night Max told his boss that he couldn't take any more and would be leaving at the end of the week. 'Ammy' appeared to agree but when the time came and he paid Max and was told that Max was going, he asked in surprise, 'What for?' Max reminded him that he had given in his notice the previous week, whereupon Ambrose roared with laughter, put his arm round Max's shoulder and said, 'You'll be with me, you mug, until you've got a beard down to your knees!' So it went on all the time, with Max giving his notice and 'Ammy' not taking it.

When they eventually came to the parting of the ways, amicably as it happens, Ambrose's farewell to the heavyweight drummer was: 'Well, goodbye Max, keep your chins up!' This farewell line was on a par with 'Ammy's' alleged greeting when Max called at his apartment in North Row, Park Lane – 'Hello Max, pull up a couple of chairs and sit down.'

I remember Max Bacon as a warm and liberal human being. On more than one occasion I witnessed his generosity after we had finished rehearsing in the BBC studios near Waterloo Station in 1935. The studios were contained in a converted railway arch in the back streets of The Cut. In the evenings, rehearsals over, we used to go for a quick drink in the public house a short way up the road. As we made our way there we often came across groups of young kids, poorly clad, many barefooted and probably neglected, running around the street. Two or three times I saw Max dig his hand into his trousers pocket and pull out a fistful of half-crowns which he gave the ragged urchins for a fish and chip supper.

As a band we made our début in films early in 1936, when we played *We're Tops on Saturday Night* in the picture *Soft Lights and Sweet Music*, perhaps Ambrose's best remembered film appearance.

12 International Fame and Wedding Bells

In September 1936 Ambrose resumed his residency at the May Fair Hotel, from where we broadcast once again every Saturday night. Early in 1937, however, 'Ammy' had talks with fellow bandleader Jack Harris which resulted in them forming a partnership to take over the management of Ciro's Club. The arrangement was that they should alternate leading a band at Ciro's for six months at a time, with Ambrose taking the first six months. Sir Francis Towle agreed to release Ambrose from his contract at the May Fair and we opened at Ciro's at the beginning of March.

In May, during the Coronation Week celebrations, the Ambrose Orchestra was invited to play for the opening of the Exposition in Paris at a super-special dance venue, the Monte Carlo Restaurant, as from the middle of June. 'Ammy', although he asked for more money than the American bands of Duke Ellington, Benny Goodman, Paul Whiteman and Eddie Duchin, was accorded this terrific honour – so by inference we were France's nomination as the world's greatest dance band! In under three months the arrangement between Jack Harris and Ambrose had hit a snag. Happily after some discussion they ironed matters out so that we were able to fulfil the engagement on the Continent.

Unfortunately, when we arrived in Paris the 250 acre Exposition site, which extended from the Place de la Concorde to the Île des Cygnes, had not been finished due to a number of strikes in the building industry. So instead of playing in the new dance venue for the Exposition – its full title in English was International Exhibition of Arts and Crafts in Modern Life – we found ourselves playing for a couple of functions at the American Embassy and for several afternoons on the bandstand in the Bois de Boulogne Gardens.

On an evening off we took the opportunity of seeing Teddy Hill's coloured American band and met the 21-year-old trumpet player John Birks Gillespie, whose penchant for clowning and general horseplay was soon to earn him the nickname 'Dizzy'.

Most of us found time in Paris to go out and enjoy ourselves in various ways. Bassist Don Stuteley and I were told of a club where fun was to be had, and although neither of us spoke the language we were determined to find out for ourselves. Setting off from our hotel one evening, Don and I approached a typically Jewish looking fellow in the street and I greeted him with 'Shalom Alachem'. Staring hard at me he responded with *'Que dites-vous là?'* Obviously I had made a faux pas! I mumbled *'Excusez-moi'* and we moved on. In time we found a guy who I was sure could help us find the way, and as soon as I uttered the magic greeting he answered in fluent Yiddish. After telling him who we were and why we were in Paris he directed us to the club. We entered through swing doors – like those one sees in old Charlie Chaplin films – with smoke pouring out, over and under them. A well-built coloured girl hustled Don and I to the bar to make sure we bought her a drink – for which I paid; and how! Through the haze of cigar and cigarette smoke I saw a room crowded with under-dressed and over-madeup women sprawling all over the men, while music blared out of an old gramophone. The girl with us was urging Don and I to go upstairs with her for 'a good time'; but when she realised that we were not too keen, she turned a bit nasty and started abusing us with some pretty ripe language, although there appeared to be plenty of other 'customers' available. A couple of tough looking gentlemen gave us threatening looks as our girl was trying to force us to accept her trade, but we made for the doors and were able to get out in one piece (each). Back at the hotel we swopped stories of the night's adventures with Joe Brannelly and Sam Browne, with whom I always shared a room on tour and who, I am sure, liked to keep an eye on me in case I strayed from the 'straight and narrow' . . . which I didn't!

Returning to England we recorded in July with our personnel now including Alfie Noakes and Tommy McQuater (t); Les Carew (tb); Albert Harris (g) and Tiny Winters (b). The recordings created an impression abroad, for the following November the band received a further international recognition when it made the headlines in *Down Beat* magazine, the American equivalent of the English *Melody Maker*. The American critic praised our recordings of *Caravan* and *Twilight in Turkey*, singling out Jack Simpson, our tympanist, and 'Billy Amstell, who plays rousing tenor solos on both sides', for special mention. The review was headed: **'ONE ENGLISH BAND CAN GIVE U.S. BANDS RUN FOR MONEY.** For Sheer Uniqueness Ambrose Band Has Edge On Many of Our Bands.' So we had made the headlines in London, Paris, and New York.

One night at Ciro's Club that July there was another Bert Barnes 'incident' when he failed to turn up on time and we had to start playing without him. 'Ammy' was very worried, and talking to no one in particular, or perhaps to the empty piano stool, whispered 'I wonder what could have happened to him?' Eventually 'Barnsey' arrived and took his place at the piano – with tears streaming down his face. We were all concerned now, none more so than the sensitive Ambrose, as we cast sympathetic glances in Barnes' direction, certain that he must have recieved bad news of some sort. The tears had diminished by the time of the interval when Don Barretto's Latin–American band took over. As we adjourned to the lower floor Bert Barnes took me aside to explain that he had only smoked too much of the 'weed', insisting that I keep the information to myself. Embarrassed by what they thought must have been a tragedy in his family, no one asked Bert any questions.

We finished at Ciro's on the 28th of the month and set off next day for Cannes where Ambrose had been asked to play at the exclusive Chez Victor, a garden restaurant on the coast. As usual, 'Ammy' had chosen a first class hotel for the band – the Hôtel Georges Cinq.

While in the South of France the Hon Mrs Cartwright, the American born

Below left:
1 Billy when young, aged 8
Right:
2 Billy aged 14 with D'Arcy's
Baby Band (end of 1925)
Below:
3 Billy aged 10 (centre) with
brother Sid (standing)

Above:
4 Jimmy Dorsey (1930)

Above left:
5 D'Arcy's Baby Band (1925–6)
Billy seated, 1st left; Sylvia Quick, 3rd left; Frank Davis (sousaphone); Violet Osborne (d)

Below left:
6 With some of Charles Watson's Band
Billy, 1st right; Jack Chapman, 2nd right

7 Bill Gerhardi (leader) at Grosvenor House Hotel (The Jack Harris Band)
Billy, middle of sax section, also included Jock Fleming (tb); Arthur Niblo (t); Gerhardi (vln);
Les Norman (as); Jack Marsh (ts); Frank Dark (sousaphone)

8 Louis de Vries and his Royal Orpheans (1931)
Mick Amstell, 1st left; Freddy Schweitzer (as); Eddie Breunner, back right; Melle Weersma,
centre back standing

9 Roy Fox Band at Monseigneur Restaurant (May 1931)

Billy, aged 19, middle sax section; Fox, front; Al Bowlly (g); Lew Stone (p); Nat Gonella, middle brass section

10 Exterior and interior of
May Fair Hotel in 1930s.
The May Fair Hotel

Right:
11 Billy, Monte Carlo, with
Bert Read, Sam Browne, Harry
Jacobsen, Joe Crossman
(10 August 1932)

Below:
12 Ambrose and Elsie Carlisle
at the May Fair Hotel (1932)
Billy talking to Danny Polo:
others in picture, Bert Barnes
(p); Dick Ball (b)
Joe Jeannette

Left:
13 American 'Blonde Bombshell' Evelyn Dall

Below right:
14 Part of a Christmas Card from Evelyn Dall to Tessa and Billy Amstell

Below left:
15 A tenor for Mr Ambrose *Mme. Yvonne*

16 Ambrose and his Orchestra 'Chez Victor', Cannes (August 1937)

Left:
17 André Dessary

Right:
18 Tessa when Billy met her on the set at Pinewood Studios in the film *Kicking the Moon Around* (1937)

Below left:
19 Billy and Tessa's wedding, June 1938
Right side of photo wearing hats, Tommy McQuater, Tiny Winters, George Chisholm

Below right:
20 Tessa and Billy (August 1938)
Melody Maker

21 Bert Ambrose

22 Group Captain Basil Embry, CO RAF Wittering

23 Sgt Amstell, RAF Wittering (1943)

24 RAF Wittering Station Dance Band (1940)
Bobby McGee, Billy, Sid Heiger, Arthur Mouncy, Tiny Winters

25   RAF Wittering Station Brass Band. CO Basil Embry, centre, Sgt Amstell holding clarinet, extreme left

26 Wartime at the London Palladium. Billy 4th from left in saxes; girl singer, Dorothy Carless

millionairess, pressed Ambrose to play at the ball she was holding at her Eden Rock residence where the Duke and Duchess of Windsor had been her guests earlier in the year. It so happened that the ball coincided with my twenty-sixth birthday, so at the end of the night I gave myself a birthday present by walking off with a couple of bottles of her champagne stowed away in my saxophone case!

It was in Cannes that we visited a club called 'The Jungle', a haunt of the gay community. What with the women dancing together, likewise the men, it was hardly surprising that when Bert Barnes and I danced together, nobody took any notice.

Music at the club was provided by a small band led by André Echian, a former member of the Ray Ventura orchestra. Although André and the boys played in fancy low-cut shirts revealing a gold chain necklance, they were dressed that way solely to blend in with the atmosphere of the place and there was not the slightest doubt in my mind that they weren't 'queers'. Just before we returned to England André, a keen yachtsman, insisted on showing me over his 30-foot craft which was moored in Cannes harbour.

Back in London we opened on 15 September at the Café de Paris, in a superb setting with an oval-shaped room lined with mirrors. The cabaret included some big names, including Vic Oliver, Beatrice Lillie and Josephine Baker who I can still picture being carried naked from the floor by six male dancers. In those days it was something of a sensation.

Round the corner in Wardour Street was one of those amusement arcades where the main attraction was the crane in a glass case inviting one, for only 6d, to win a desirable prize. Arthur Lally had the knack of operating the crane so as to pick up the star prize – in this instance an alarm clock which Max Bacon had his eye on. Max soon persuaded Arthur to do a deal with him; so the next evening Arthur, having successfully applied his expertise, popped into the bandroom to give a delighted Max his prize, but without letting on that he had set the alarm for 2am. Max proudly placed the clock beside his drum kit on the bandstand – and sure enough, as we stood to play the National Anthem at the end of the evening's entertainment, the alarm went off loud and clear! Martin Poulsen, the suave manager, appeared stunned as he looked down from the balcony overlooking the bandstand, and the patrons were bewildered as we played louder and louder to try to drown the noise. The Yacht Club Boys, a popular American singing group of the time who were appearing in the cabaret, reckoned it was the funniest practical joke they had seen in a night spot.

During the period September 1936 to late October 1937 we recorded no fewer than 125 titles. The excellent Albert Harris remained on guitar since Joe Brannelly was very busy as a band manager. The saxophone section stayed as it was and had been since the autumn of 1933 – Danny, Sid, Joe and I. We were rehearsed until we were 'as one man', for Danny would have it no other way. Two of our outstanding recordings of this time were *Deep Henderson* and *Cotton Pickers' Congregation* recorded on 8 July 1937, both scored by Sid Phillips and the latter composed by him.

At the end of October Ambrose refused to renew his contract with Decca on the terms offered, which called for a reduction in fees on account of the depressed state of the recording industry. Yet our band alone had made the equivalent of ten LPs in just over a year. We were not to resume recording until October 1938.

1937 was a very busy year in the film studios. In March the band appeared, along with other variety attractions, in *Calling All Stars*; a little later we made a 'short' which included Sid Phillips's *Night Ride*, and early in November work began at the Pinewood studios on *Kicking the Moon Around* in which Ambrose was to have a reasonable sized acting rôle. The making of this last film was to have a direct effect on my then bachelor status.

Late one afternoon, after we had finished filming for the day, trombonist Les Carew came to see me accompanied by a lovely grey-eyed girl with blonde hair and asked if I would give her a lift to Neasden station on my way home. I did not have to be asked twice! She, too, was connected with the picture, as stand-in for the famous Florence Desmond, and had met Les two years previously at the Twickenham studios when he was with Jack Hylton filming *She Shall Have Music*, in which she had played the part of a showgirl. Her name was Tessa Gee, and the following evening when giving her another lift to the station, I learned that she lived in Queens Park, which I passed on my way to Stepney. A couple of days later I arranged to meet her at 8am the next morning near her home, so that we could drive to the studios together. I regret to say that I was two and a half hours late: I had overslept! When I finally met up with Tessa at Pinewood she told me she had waited as long as she dared before making her way by rail and that on the journey she had heard that there had been a major road accident on my route and feared the worst. I was not the most popular chap at Pinewood that day and Tessa did not make any more arrangements for me to drive her to work.

Towards the end of the filming we started dating. I took her to tea and to the cinema and from then on we began 'courting'. Our courtship was usually restricted to Sundays, since during the week Tessa was working as a model for hair stylists, while I was often in the recording studios by day and playing six nights a week at the Café de Paris, although I usually managed to telephone her at her mother's home in Brondesbury Road most nights during the band's break. After my first visit there she said her mother had told her not to kiss me as she was sure I had tuberculosis, largely because I had what we used to call 'night club tan'! Tessa still remembers her first visit to my home, for she made a most undignified entrance by tripping over a rug in the hall and falling flat on her face! Just before we met she had the choice of working on one of two films being made at the same time. As she travelled to Pinewood on the first morning she read her 'stars' on the train and discovered that she was about to meet someone who would change the whole course of her life. She is inclined still to believe that her future was determined by celestial bodies!

Tessa and I became engaged while I was working at the Café de Paris and I was still there when we were married on 19 June 1938 at the Brondesbury '*shul*' (synagogue), Dyan Lazarus officiating. Tessa, who looked – and still is – beautiful, is slightly taller than me, but she wore low heels and I had elevators in my shoes! The whole band was at the wedding and couldn't make out why I seemed the taller of the two. Only Les Carew guessed the reason.

As it is the custom to cover the head when in *shul*, the non-Jewish boys were obliged to buy hats. Les, George Chisholm, Joe Jeannete, Tommy McQuater and Tiny Winters, who all looked most elegant in their hats, offered to sell them to me afterwards – wholesale of course!

The reception, held in the First Avenue Hotel in Holborn, became a very lively affair as the hours wore on. Evelyn Dall and 'Ammy' were enjoying themselves until, during the *Lambeth Walk*, someone kicked Ambrose up the seat of the pants, which neither he nor I thought particularly funny. Fortunately, David Godfrey, an early friend of Tessa's from the Young Israel Club, came to the rescue with some of his humorous patter. Tessa and I booked into the Regent Palace Hotel for the night, before leaving for a week's honeymoon in Battle – it sounds a funny place to begin a married life! It was a rare hot summer night and with the hotel windows flung wide open, we got little peace from the band at a nearby night-spot.

Max Goldberg and Tommy McQuater were also married in a year when everything seemed to be happening, including an outburst by Ambrose in the *Melody Maker* in February. The paper reported that whole sections of the orchestra had appeared under the names of other leaders who only worked with scratch combinations on jobs that would otherwise fall to established bands. Ambrose was quoted as saying: 'I have warned every man that if he works sessions without my permission, he will be fired incontinently without warning and irrevocably. I am going to the extent of having watchers on duty at known sessions to see if any of my men are on them . . . I am certainly not going to maintain the best possible instrumentalists just so as a lot of West End orchestrators can gather them up from time to time and snatch engagements at a cheaper price because they don't have to pay out weekly salaries. I have already issued my ultimatum because I understood that some of my band were going to do a broadcast with Lew Stone, who has no dance band available. I am sorry I have to take this step in a case in which so well-respected and right-thinking a fellow as Lew Stone is concerned and I wish it were anyone else but I have delayed my decision too long and now I will make no exception in anybody's favour. If it means I have to recruit an entirely new band I will do it. I pay top money and I now demand exclusive service . . .'

A week later 'Ammy' fired Eric Breeze for disobeying his instructions. Later on, so far as I can recall, he did not enforce his rule so stringently, although he still didn't like what was happening.

The first time I played at Buckingham Palace was when Ambrose was summoned to provide the music for the Derby Ball on 1 June 1938. The Duke of Kent had heard Evelyn Dall singing with the band at the Café de Paris and had said to Bert one evening, 'Ambrose, I want you to bring Miss Dall to our dance.' 'Ammy' had to agree although he was uneasy as no dance band vocalist had ever performed there before. On the night, we had been playing for nearly an hour with no vocals and Evelyn was nagging Bert about when she was to sing. Finally, he plucked up courage and said to her: 'Do the next number – *Nice Work if You Can Get it.*' So at last out over the ballroom rolled her thick American accent. All heads were turned at once upwards to our position on the balcony. Bert was very apprehensive, especially when she finished and there was complete momentary silence. Then the Queen applauded and was followed by tremendous applause from all round the ballroom. Was Ambrose relieved!

The next day there was no mention of him or the band in the newspapers; but Evelyn's picture was plastered all over the front page of the *Daily Mirror* with the headline: **EVELYN DALL FIRST CROONER AT BUCKINGHAM PALACE**.

'I was burned up,' said 'Ammy'. 'I thought they might have mentioned the man she worked for!'

What really caught my eye that night in those magnificent surroundings was the most beautiful chandelier with its attractive crystal baubles which gave off many lovely colours. As the Queen took the floor for her favourite dance – the Viennese waltz – I took note of the ladies' stunning gowns – for Tessa's benefit of course.

The following day, as a member of the Embassy Eight, I played at the American Embassy at the behest of Lady Nancy Astor, for the benefit of some 25 or so US Navy personnel. There was a bar and a buffet but no dancing. We played the numbers requested by the Navy lads – *Chicago*, *I'm Coming Virginia*, *You Took Advantage of Me* and so on – and they were an enthusiastic audience. Danny Polo, Joe Brannelly and Max Goldberg spoke the language of North America of course, and felt very much at home. I think I must have been too, for after about three hours I had acquired an American accent. The charming and fascinating Lady Astor was full of life and most popular with the Navy boys. Just before we finished someone gave her a chair to stand on while she addressed the guests. She then thanked the band – I wonder if she ever knew how much we ourselves had enjoyed the evening. She left to three rousing cheers.

When the Café de Paris job ended the band took a short holiday and then toured from the autumn of 1938 to the early spring of 1939. A young girl singer had joined the band in the spring of '37 and recorded with us many times, gradually establishing herself. Within a few short years she was to become known as 'The Forces Sweetheart' and to marry one of our saxophonists, Harry Lewis. This of course was Vera Lynn, now Dame Vera. She shared the vocal work with Evelyn Dall and former Roy Fox singer Denny Dennis who had joined in September 1938 as replacement for Sam Browne. Other changes included Ivor Mairants on guitar, Joe Crossman back on alto and Archie Craig on trumpet.

One night when we were appearing at the London Palladium, Vera Lynn was indisposed and a wag from the audience called out – 'Where's Vera?' Quick as a flash Ambrose retorted, 'She's washing her hair!'

In October 1938 Ambrose resolved his differences with Decca and we resumed recording sessions that month. We went into the studios about once a fortnight, so that by early April 1939 we had recorded a further 60 titles. My own composition, *Tootin' Around*, on which I was well featured on tenor, was one of that 60. Our tour had come to an end in April and as Ambrose had no residency to take up through the summer months, I returned to Jack Harris, this time to play at the London Casino. I was with Jack for three and a half months, at the same time continuing as a member of Ambrose's recording band.

Just before rejoining Jack Harris, Geraldo invited me to appear on 2 April as one of the guest artists on one of his popular Sunday Night Swing Club concerts in St Martin's Theatre, off Shaftesbury Avenue. Other guests I met there included the immortal Thomas 'Fats' Waller, Adelaide Hall and George Shearing. Those concerts featured the 'Heralds of Swing', a ten-piece outfit, and that evening more than half of them were Ambrose instrumentalists plus Sam Browne and Eddie Pola as compères.

13 The London Casino, the May Fair and the end of an era

When the London Casino reopened on 12 April 1939, Jack Harris was back in form directing his own band there and also being the personal manager of violinist Hugo Rignold's band, which he put in especially to accompany the floor show.

The Jack Harris orchestra was generally reckoned to be the finest ballroom band of the time in this country and had been one of the hits of the 'Jazz Jamboree' held at the end of March. There was a number of Canadians in the lineup, including pianist Jack Penn, who was also staff arranger, violinist Bill Schneiderman, Jack's right-hand man, and trumpeter Max Goldberg. There was also first alto Harry Karr who had studied with the famous American saxophone virtuoso Rudy Wiedoeft. He was also a very fine performer on flute and clarinet, and had been introduced over here by E. O. (Poggy) Pogson, himself a reed player in much demand. Another 'Canadian connection' was David Miller who was engaged to compère our broadcasts. Among other members of our group was ex-Ambrose trombonist Eric Breeze and violinist Max Jaffa. Sharing the vocals were the beautiful Pat Taylor of the divine figure and Hughie Diamond, a vigorous young Scot, more than six feet tall, full of zest and the possessor of a powerful voice, which did not need the assistance of a microphone then and still doesn't today when he sings to fans at the annual meeting of 'Memory Lane'. In his time at the London Casino, Hughie attracted a good deal of attention by appearing in 'loud' clothes. Some of the band were liable to take the 'mickey' out of him because of it and so aroused his considerable temper. I sometimes had to step in to calm him by pointing out that if he ignored them they would soon drop the subject!

Jack Harris, since leaving the Embassy Club, had gone flat out to win a reputation for leading the best 'hot' band in Britain. In the opinion of many he had now achieved that ambition. It was reported in the music press that our relays to the States had done much to raise the prestige of British dance bands there and in fact compare favourably with the Ambrose recordings that had been heard there. It was always Jack's ambition to have a better band than Ambrose, so the likes of Max Goldberg, Eric Breeze and myself were always assured of a job! In my short time with the band we recorded 26 titles, including much admired versions of Sid Phillips's *Swing Band* and *Mr Reynard's Nightmare*.*

In June 1939 *Melody Maker* enthused: 'Harris stands in front of 15 of the best musicians in the country while they play half an hour of jazz.'

When our engagement at the London Casino came to an end we went on a short

---

*At recording sessions Jack would sometimes reach for the nearest violin and begin playing, surprising Max Jaffa and the other violinists.

summer tour 'by public demand' as they say. During our run at the Coventry Hippodrome, Tessa, who came on tour with me whenever possible, and I were taking an early evening stroll before the show when we came upon an ugly crowd in the town centre. In the middle of it was Hughie Diamond being jostled and generally man-handled. People were shouting at him, and the thoroughly dishevelled Hughie was shouting back at them – 'I did'nee dee it: I did'nee dee it!' Tessa and I managed to intervene and explain that Hughie was a singer with our band that was currently appearing at their theatre. What had happened was that our young Scottish vocalist had been mistaken for an IRA terrorist! At this time the IRA were blowing up post office letter boxes in various parts of England and somehow the local people had taken Hughie's Scots accent for an Irish one!

The clouds of war were gathering fast when I rejoined Ambrose. Shortly after hostilities had broken out the band went on tour and on 11 October, and while we were playing a week in Glasgow, I received news that my father was very seriously ill. I rushed back to London by train not knowing that he had already died from pneumonia half an hour before I left Glasgow.

Ambrose returned to the May Fair Hotel just before Christmas and I continued with him until the summer of 1940 when I volunteered to join the RAF. So ended an era. As I left the band I realised that when I joined in 1931 I was the youngest of Ambrose's musicians, and so I was when I left nine years later. Joe Jeannette and Max Bacon were there when I arrived – and they were still there when I left. I had always been happy working with Bert Ambrose and I thought him a good boss. He was proud of his band and of his arrangers, who knew exactly who they were writing for and what was required of them. The band carried no passengers and I believe that the LPs that have been released over the past 20 years or so clearly demonstrate the superiority of the Ambrose orchestra over other British dance bands of the day – and over a good few American ones too.

I have often been asked where Ambrose came upon his signature tune *When Day Is Done*. It was originally called *Madonna*, written and published in Vienna, and arrived in this country at around the time Paul Whiteman was touring here. 'The King of Jazz' as Hollywood was to name him – he was never that – took the number back to the States with him as *Panama*. It returned to England shortly afterwards with the title we have known it by ever since. Ambrose adopted it because he thought it the most appropriate signature tune for his Saturday night broadcasts.

I took my leave of the May Fair Hotel with an incredible wealth of happy memories and the knowledge that I had made something in the region of 1000 recordings and nearly half as many broadcasts as part of the famous Ambrose Orchestra.

The Battle of Britain was only a few weeks away . . .

14   1284755 in the Royal Air Force

On 19 May 1940 I wrote to the Central Band of the RAF at Uxbridge volunteering to join the service with a 12-piece band. I was notified at the end of the month that the recruiting programme allowed for only combinations of five and if I could provide two such units it might be possible to post them to neighbouring stations so that they could give concerts at both combining as a ten-piece band. Accordingly, an audition was arranged with Wing Commander O'Donnell, the Director of Music of the Royal Air Force.

When we arrived at Uxbridge I drove straight through the main gate (the barrier was in the up position!). I heard a lot of shouting but being a mere civilian, I didn't understand that we were being challenged. It was lucky that the man on guard behind a machine gun was Eric Breeze, and he recognised me. Strictly according to regulations, he should have shot me! The other musicians in our party were, Jack Nathan, the former Roy Fox pianist and arranger; trumpet men Chick Smith and Arthur Mouncey, reed players Hughie Tripp and Harry Smith, drummers Sid Heiger and Tom Webster, and trombonists Bruce Campbell and Abe Walters. We passed the audition with ease but lost Harry Smith to The King's Royal Rifles and Tom Webster to O'Donnell's main orchestra, while Australian Abe Walters was advised to report to Australia House. It was decided that Jack Nathan should take a five piece outfit to RAF Cottismore and I a similar one to RAF Wittering in Northamptonshire. As the two camps were only some 20 miles apart, the idea was that we could get together, as had been intimated in my original notification; but in fact we only played together once in two years. My band consisted of Arthur Mouncey, Sid Heiger and two from the musicians 'pool' – pianist Bobby McGee and a bassist called Fred Gittens – but Tiny Winters to you!

So on 12 August 1940, No 1284755 officially joined the RAF. One of the attesting officers was Teddy Summerfield, who used to fix me up with film dates at Elstree and Pinewood before the war. Teddy signalled for me to stay behind after the attestation and I stood to attention not knowing whether I should salute or not. 'Relax, for Christ's sake!' Teddy growled. 'How are you, Billy?' I replied that I was not sure, as indeed I wasn't – that is until he asked me, 'Would you like a ten hour pass?' Naturally I jumped at that, informing him that I had left my car in the car park – some nerve, I guess! There can't have been many airmen who joined in style in those days!

When I returned home, my arm painful from injections and the regulation issue boots playing hell with my feet, I think Tessa was more upset than I was. I may not have been much of an RAFVR, but the heart was willing. By midnight I was back at Uxbridge to find that I was most unpopular with the corporal in charge of the billet for not only was I a musician but I had been granted a pass without his knowledge. The next morning I was ordered to report to a room where two officers were seated, and in my ignorance I saluted the Warrant Officer instead of the commissioned officer. Of course my hostile corporal made the most of this little faux pas. The officer then gave me a 'pep' talk about Winston Churchill's recent broadcast speech . . . that every man must do his duty, etc . . . Well – it was all a little too much for me; as Spike Milligan would have said, 'it went in one head and out of the other'.

For the next few days, as a pleasant change from the luxuriant environment of the May Fair Hotel, I found myself cleaning out the latrines. Thankfully, we were soon posted officially to the Central Band. As we fell in one parade, the hawk-eyed Drum Major Sutheron spotted how extra-smart drummer Ray Ellington was dressed. 'That's a very nice jacket you're wearing, Ellington . . . one pace forward . . . turn round,' commanded Sutheron. Some tailor had made a magnificent job of altering Ray's jacket. 'My word, those shoulders are perfect – luvverly work.' Then in a voice that could have offended the ears as far away as Hendon, Sutheron bellowed: 'Take it orf!'

When the posting to Wittering came through, Sid Heiger and I made the journey in his car and I remembered to take along with us some special arrangements Ambrose had kindly given me, although I could not really use them for a band of five. When we arrived Sid parked his car outside Station HQ and we, being as green as the grass which surrounded the building, walked across the lawn. Instantly a voice thundered a 'Get off the grass!' plus an expletive which went a long way towards extending my RAF vocabulary. This roar of thunder was delivered by Physical Training Instructor, Sgt Spalton who, we later discovered was not really such a bad chap – he liked our music!

After three weeks at Wittering I found a house in nearby Easton-on-the-Hill that had a vacancy for a married couple. I arranged to bring Tessa up from London and applied for permission to live out of camp. In fact we were far from happy in these lodgings and never settled in. Luckily, within six weeks or so, one of the lads put me onto a little cottage in Easton which stood empty. The owner, Mrs. Kisbee, who lived next door, agreed to rent it to us and for the next three years it provided to be an ideal home for Tessa, her mother, myself, our cat, dog . . . and pet jackdaw!

Our band quickly became popular at the various mess dances – not least because we were known to be former Ambrose and/or Lew Stone musicians. Shortly after I had been promoted to corporal and we were engaged to play for a dance in the Sergeants' Mess, and as the band was setting up the Mess President walked in armed with a large box of chalk which he proceeded to throw, far more than liberally, over the floor. In fact there was nowhere he didn't throw it! The result was that the dancers were waltzing in a cloud, with boots and shoes – and even our instruments – all nearly snow-white. Meekly I told the sergeant that the stuff would choke us all, but his three stripes chose to ignore my two! How different it was later on when I played there as Sgt in charge of the band. The same fellow started with the damned chalk again, until I yelled, 'We don't need any of that bloody stuff, Sarge!' 'OK,' he replied mildly. I thought at once that three stripes are so much better than two!

I believe that those three stripes had the effect of turning me from an introvert into an extrovert. I had suffered from shyness in my childhood and beyond, probably from the way my mother used to brag about her children. I could hear her saying . . . 'My Mick, he's such a handsome fellow . . . Rosie, so beautiful . . . Sid, so tall and good-looking . . . and Billy? . . . he's a good boy.' I saw myself as a short, ordinary lad, unmistakably Jewish in appearance. When I discovered I could play the saxophone, I dedicated myself to doing just that; but I had little conversation apart from music and the longer I remained silent the more difficult it became for me to say anything. I remained basically shy and introverted . . . until those three stripes!

We were allowed civilian guests at the camp dances, and on one such night Tessa was dancing on the very crowded floor as we played a waltz for the Lucky Spot Prize. I gave Sid Heiger the signal to hit the cymbal and immediately the spotlight had to beam straight onto my wife! Hurriedly I ordered the band to play on – well, no one was going to believe that it was pure coincidence.

At Wittering my first Commanding Officer, Harry Broadhurst (later Sir Harry) gave me a free hand to organise the entertainment, which I did nearly every night in a separate mess. Our five-piece band also played some gigs out of camp and, becoming ambitious, Bobby McGee and I wrote some interesting arrangements from recordings, such as *Special Delivery Stomp* and *Pastel Blue* (both by Artie Shaw) and *Sm-o-o-th One*, *Good Enough to Keep* and *Opus* $1/2$ (all by Benny Goodman). The popular songs of the day were also included. The 151 (Night Fighter) Squadron and Spitfire crews' special requests were *In the Mood* and *Woodchopper's Ball* which were played over and over again.

Another who helped organising the RAF dances at Wittering was Squadron Leader 'Admin' Morice who was something of a man about town and frequented such night-spots as Ciro's, the Embassy and the May Fair. He remembered Arthur Mouncey and I from former days and when I needed a lift into Stamford, some three or four miles away, to pick up the current popular tunes from Claypoles music shop, he would provide it. It was at Claypoles that I met Mary Burton who ordered the music I needed when it was not in stock. Tessa and I would often meet at the music shop and we became friends with Mary and her husband Reg, an RAF rear gunner.

Miss Prior, the secretary of the Stamford Social Club, arranged many gigs for our little band. We were engaged to play every week at 25 shillings a time, which handsomely supplemented our RAF pay of half a crown a day. During my two and a half years at Wittering the visitors to the camp dances enjoyed the band so much that we were invited to play in various places. I recall a gig at the Grand Hotel, Leicester, the Town Hall, Peterborough, the Corn Exchange, Wisbech as well as many for the Oakham Cricket Club socials. For this outside work I usually employed the car hire firm run by Reg Cowley, whose spacious vintage car could easily accommodate the five of us plus instruments. Practically all the functions we played at were put on to raise money for the various War Effort charities. Much of the money made from the RAF dances was paid into the PSI (President Services Institute) who in turn footed the bill. The entertainments officer, Flight Lieutenant Miller, decided that our appearance would be enhanced if we desported ourselves in blue blazers, grey flannels and shoes for the camp dances.

Another welcome little 'perk' came our way when Bert Bullimore, leader of the trumpet section in Jack Payne's band, obtained permission from our CO for the band to play at the Jazz Jamborees in London. This brought some extra leave plus four shillings and sixpence subsistence allowance. (Bert was lead trumpet when I later joined Stanley Black's orchestra at the BBC.) A further 'perk' was recording in the Drury Lane Theatre for the Overseas Recorded Broadcasts Service (ORBS) six 15-minute programmes in the 'Swingtime' series. I recall one Jazz Jamboree in 1941 when Carl Barriteau re-formed Ken ('Snakehips') Johnson's orchestra. I was in the saxophone section with Carl, Aubrey Frank and George Roberts; Kenny Baker was one of the trumpets along with Leslie 'Jiver' Hutchinson and Dave Wilkins.

My brother Mick and his pal, fellow saxophonist Harry Hines (later to become known as Dr Crock of the Crackpots) paid Tessa and I a visit in our little two up and two down in Easton when, as members of Maurice Winnick's band they were playing a week in Peterborough. As they had not been on an RAF camp before, I took them on a tour which included the hangers where Spitfires were serviced. Of course, they both wanted to sit in a 'Spit' – first Harry and then Mick – and as they did so the air became full of the choicest RAF language as a Flight Sergeant mechanic spotted what we were doing. I was responsible for bringing two unauthorised civilians onto the airfield and the F/Sgt was advising me that I was likely to find myself 'doing time' in Shepton Mallet or some other equally attractive 'glass house'. After the very thick air had cleared 'Flight' reminded me that it was extremely fortunate that no officer was around to observe my breach of security. I was thankful for that and promised to play the F/Sgt's favourite tune, *In The Mood* at the next dance (when did we not feature that number!). I introduced Mick and Harry, who produced two complimentary tickets for their concert, to meet Maurice Winnick and the boys in the band. 'Flight' was delighted while I reflected how easily I could have dropped a real clanger through being thoughtless. Earlier I had taken Tessa out to where an extended runway had been built to accommodate Lancaster bombers in the event of an emergency landing. We were looking over a fully bomb-loaded Lancaster when I suddenly asked myself what we were doing there and quickly led Tessa away. The camp suffered bombings from time to time and when there was an air raid during a dance, most people got 'pissed' to ease their worries. On one such night, at a dance in the Sergeants' Mess, a friend of mine was nearly crying on my shoulder that after the war was over, he would have to return to his wife. That was his BIG worry!

15   Sound of Brass

During his time as Officer Commanding RAF Station Wittering, Basil Embry (later Air Marshal Sir Basil Embry, KCB, KBE, DSO, DFC, AFC) was responsible for the formation of the 21-piece Station Brass Band. I was made Sergeant in charge. We needed a quantity of instruments, so I suggested that we visit Boosey & Hawkes in Regent Street, where I was well known to all the staff. In fact, a year or so earlier Boosey & Hawkes had featured me in one of their advertisements as playing their make of clarinet and saxophone, while Jeffrey Hawkes had been one of the regulars at the May Fair Hotel. We purchased £500 worth of instruments but they never so much as offered me a reed in appreciation or 'commission'!

As part of the Spitfire Week activities the CO gave permission for the band to march to Easton-on-the-Hill and Stamford to play for the townsfolk. At Stamford we halted outside the local cinema, formed ourselves into a circle and commenced to play. During a very loud passage a nearby horse-drawn cart bolted up the main street and out of sight. Station Warrant Officer Culf, who lived locally and was one of the crowd, always maintained that the horse bolted because of all the wrong notes we played! He was a nice enough fellow – off camp – but he didn't know a crochet from his elbow.

One afternoon during the gas-drill exercise I was in the bandroom sorting out some music when I heard what sounded like someone playing the piano with his feet. I investigated and found some 'erk' – I'll call him ''Iggins'' – wearing a gas mask and extracting some pretty awful music from the piano with his far from nimble fingers. 'What the hell do you think you're doing?' I asked him. 'Don't be angry, Sarge – it soothes me nerves,' came the reply. My anger quickly turned to pity: he appeared such a forlorn and pathetic character – so I left him to his own devices. Later on that afternoon, with the brass band playing and the parade ground full of all available officers, Air Chief Marshal Lord Trenchard took the march past. Suddenly, an airman broke ranks, strode up to the ACM and asked: 'Can you tell me the way to the NAAFI, corporal?' To my astonishment, it was the piano-pounding 'Iggins! There was an immediate flurry of urgent activity which ended in SWO Culf marching 'Iggins off to be examined by the Station Medical Officer who, having listened amazed to what had just taken place out on the parade ground, proceeded to examine the poor 'erk'. Apparently there was nothing physically wrong with 'Iggins, so the MO decided to test his mental state by setting him a series of arithmetical problems, chalked on a blackboard, all of which the 'erk' solved without difficulty. The MO became frustrated as he felt sure there must be some grounds for recommending a discharge. Later on, when I tackled this character on how he managed to solve mathematical problems so easily, he said it was a trick he had learned from *Old Moore's Almanack*! However, within a matter of weeks, 'Iggins fell [or was he pushed?] from the tailboard of a 'liberty-waggon' outside the guardroom, sustaining severe injuries to his back, following which the MO finally recommended him for a medical discharge. Before 'Iggins departed the camp I let him play the piano for the last time. I ignored the chap's fractured playing, for I had learned that he was heartbroken at leaving the RAF which had, for perhaps the only time in his life, provided him with accommodation, clothing, regular meals, and, not least, companionship.

Walking through the camp one evening I was surprised to have a baby jackdaw perch itself on my shoulder, squawking merrily. He accompanied me noisily to my car and showed no sign of flying off after I had unlocked it. I was on my way home to Easton with a Sleeping Out Pass and as the bird was still attaching itself to me, I placed him in the boot of the car. Arriving at the cottage I took the still squawking jackdaw indoors to show to Tessa and my mother-in-law. He very soon made himself at home, and became very friendly with our cat, which we had brought with us from London, and also with the puppy I had acquired from a corporal on the camp. Naturally we named the bird 'Jackie'. We allowed him to fly free but he always returned to the cottage around twilight. One of his favourite calling places was our local, the Exeter Arms, which was nearly opposite the cottage. I was told that once inside he would strut along the bar, taking a sip out of the pint pots. Until I heard about this, I was always puzzled by the smell of beer on his breath on his return home some nights. Another place he frequented was the village school where unfortunately he disrupted the classes, although he naturally amused the children. On more than one occasion the headmistress sent Tessa a note requesting her to call to collect 'Jackie'.

When I was allocated some petrol coupons for leave we all set off for our London home. On the journey I pulled into a filling station where the attendant gave me a pitying look as he noticed the three of us in the car accompanied by a cat, a dog, and a jackdaw. On arrival home I let 'Jackie' fly free until dusk and then, as I usually did at Easton, walked the street with my crooked arm raised, calling 'Jackie, Jackie'. He was enjoying his freedom after the drive and I had to call out several times. A lady who saw and heard me from an open window shook her head sympathetically exclaiming, 'Poor lad; poor lad'. I felt most embarrassed and foolish, which I probably looked, until 'Jackie' at last homed in on me.

Back in Easton once more, the jackdaw was behaving mischievously and displeased our landlady next door by taking a pair of scissors from her dressing table as well as committing one or two other 'crimes' of theft. So with heavy hearts Tessa and I decided to set him free at the camp next time I was due for some leave. This we did: on our return I learned that 'Jackie' had been up to his tricks. Jackdaws are by nature attracted to colourful objects and he had flown off with an engagement ring from the WAAF quarters, pecked the eye of a WAAF sergeant in the mess and stolen a ten shilling note from our mess. We had 'Jackie' for more than four months, and every minute was a joy – at least to Tessa and I.

As the anniversary of my father's death drew near I felt I should pay a visit to a *shul*. The nearest one, I was told, was in Peterborough, some ten miles distant. My 'right-hand man' in the band, Arthur Mouncey kindly agreed to accompany me. This was our first year in Northamptonshire and Peterborough was a new town to both of us. We walked round the streets for some hours in search of the *shul* but without success. As we grew more and more tired with our feet protesting inside our RAF boots, I wished I had asked Rev Levy, during his last visit to the camp, the exact location of the *shul*. We returned to Wittering disappointed and nursing sore feet! I made my way to the bandroom, which was also used by Padre Mossop for storing his robes, prayer books and wine. He was there when I entered and as he noticed my dejection I told him about our abortive trip. 'Well then,' he announced to my surprise, 'we shall say prayers in here.' He reached for his prayer book and turned to the appropriate page as I, all five feet three inches tall, stood facing him, well over six feet; and we prayed together. I was deeply grateful to this Church of England padre for saying *Kaddish* (memorial prayers) with a Jewish lad. On Rev Levy's next visit to the camp I told him the story whereupon he sought out Padre Mossop and warmly thanked him.

On cold Sunday mornings I would light the fire for Padre Mossop, put out his robes and prepare the wine for the Communion, at the same time, I must confess, warming myself with a little nip. (Well, it would be seven o'clock on a winter morning and there would be this bottle of wine staring me in the face!) I would then muster up the brass band for Church Parade. The CO insisted that the *Red Flag* be played on Church Parade. The first time he ordered me to play it, I was not at all sure I had heard him correctly. Noticing my uncertainty he repeated the order, adding, 'It makes the men march that much better!'

Once a month the Station Dance Band played during dinner in the Officers' Mess where the tiny balcony was just big enough for five of us. Following the meal, and immediately before the port was served, it was our custom to play *Roast Beef of Old England* – known to the band as 'Salt Beef of Old England' – which was always enthusiastically and rowdily appreciated by the whole mess. Then, as laid down in King's Regulations, the 'bandmaster' took port with the Commanding Officer, although I somehow doubt that when this particular regulation was drafted, anyone envisaged the 'bandmaster' being the leader of a five-piece dance band! Nonetheless, I took my seat next to the CO, Basil Embry, and over the port asked him if the music was to his liking and not so loud as to interfere with the dinner and the conversation. He always assured me that they were all enjoying our playing, usually suggesting that I 'pep it up' when I rejoined the boys after finishing my port. He was at all times most courteous towards me during our five or ten minutes together, after which I would ask to be excused as I did not wish to abuse the privilege – even though another glass or two of that excellent port would have been welcome.

After playing *In The Mood* (yet again!) and other popular tunes of the day, we featured some traditional Scottish music, whereupon the CO and a lot of the younger officers, including F/Lt 'Cats Eye' Stevens DSO, DFC and Bar, mounted the mess tables for a little 'dancing'. Not knowing the difference, and probably not even caring, the CO performed an Irish Jig to a Scottish Reel, and the other officers followed suit. It was not long before the sauce bottles hit the ceiling . . .

Our Commanding Officer, author of the book *Wingless Victory*, had been shot down over France early in the war and taken prisoner. He did, however, manage to escape and taking a route through Spain he finally made it back to England. His first posting was to RAF Wittering where it was strongly rumoured that, when a young captured German pilot was brought to the guard room, clicking his heels and giving the Nazi salute, Wing Commander Embry, because of his hatred of all Nazis and without batting an eyelid landed him a sock on the jaw . . . and walked out!

16 Flying High –
and Low

It was in the late 1920s that I first had the urge to take to the air – with a five shilling 'flip' down at Brighton. The flight lasted for only about five to six minutes, with the pilot and four passengers cramped into the tiny cabin of the 'plane. I found it such a thrill that soon afterwards I simply had to have another flip, after which I determined to learn to fly myself as soon as I had an opportunity. This did not come until 1934 when a friend of mine, Bob Wise, a qualified pilot and in his time a saxophonist with Carroll Gibbons, Jack Harris and Ray Noble, invited me to Croydon Aerodrome for a lesson. After about ten minutes in the air, to my astonishment he handed the control over to me and for the next 20 minutes or so I was banking left . . . banking right . . . while Bob sat there with his hands raised aloft to show me I was in full control. I really believed that I had an aptitude for flying and the following week he gave me another lesson. On this occasion Bob showed me the plane and sports car belonging to bandleader Billy Cotton that were parked in a corner of the hangar. Bill was a man of many parts; he served in the Army and then the RFC in the Great War, had been a bus conductor, a professional footballer, and then a racing driver, as well as leader of a top class band. I knew his boys thought highly of him and he was much respected in our profession. Pressure of work, both at home and abroad, did not allow me the time for more flying lessons, and soon after the start of World War II Bob Wise joined the RAF as an instructor.

In the early years of the war, I did get the opportunity to have a go in a Link Trainer. The purpose of this piece of equipment was to teach the pupil to fly by instruments while at the controls with all light blacked out. After a few minutes the instructor knocked on the dome, and as I opened up informed me that I had 'crashed'! I enjoyed all the flights I have ever made and have never experienced nerves or air sickness.

Shortly after my experience with the Link Trainer I applied to remuster to air-crew duties. The monotony of playing *In the Mood* and *Woodchopper's Ball* again and yet again, so many times every week, was getting to me and I felt I had to do something more positive. I began thinking about Bob Wise and other fellow musicians like Max Jaffa, Frank Weir, Alfie Kahn and Jim Easton who were among the air-crews I admired – not forgetting 'Cats Eye' Stevens. It was when the station dance band went out to the dispersal points to play for fighter pilots that I first met him. He would often help get our instruments out of the car and he couldn't resist tapping away on the drums as he did it. He certainly seemed to nurse a hatred of the Nazis: his wife and child had been killed in an air raid. I was honoured when he gave me his cockpit seat as a keepsake, although I later decided that it should really be in the RAF museum at Hendon. I presented it to them and the facts are recorded there.

F/Lt Stevens was killed in December 1941 during a Night Intruder sortie over Occupied Europe. In that year he had destroyed at least fourteen enemy aircraft by night, including two in the London area which he had chased for over 100 miles. He was, it seems, given *carte blanche* to engage in a ruthless pursuit of the enemy, anytime . . . anywhere . . .

In due course I was sent to Grantham for medical examination, to assess my fitness for flying duties. There was no problem until my left eye was tested: this proved to be slightly stigmatic and my hopes were dashed. The MO put his hand on my shoulder and tried to reassure me that I was 'doing a worthwhile job anyway'. This was not much consolation. I tried to concentrate on my music and was grateful to have the benefit of continuing to play at the Jazz Jamborees and for ORBS. But despite these perks I was still feeling rather depressed – and then I developed an aching in both knees. The station MO prescribed a treatment of heat and embrocation; but that only resulted in my legs swelling up to three times their normal size!

A short spell in station sickquarters was followed by a transfer to Bracebridge Military Hospital near Lincoln, early in 1943. There 593 M&B, the drug that had saved Winston Churchill, restored my poisoned system and I was granted sick leave – after, that is, recovering from a form of dermatitis and a boil in the groin!

Meanwhile, things had been happening at RAF Wittering, not least the posting of our CO, Basil Embry. This was followed by an Air Ministry decision to dispense with the station brass band while retaining our five-piece unit until posting us to Sunburgh in the Shetland Isles. Arthur, Tiny, Bobby and Sid preceded me to Sunburgh while I finished my sick leave. I soon followed, making the journey north via Invergordon, where the transit camp had all the appearance of a POW camp. I found it exceptionally cheerless. Once inside, however, the canteen ladies, noticing that I didn't look the fittest man around, provided me with hot soup and showed me where to collect blankets etc. Each Nissen hut contained four bunks – two up and two down – and having been allocated an upper bunk I lost no time turning in after the long journey, not caring that there were no lights and that a damp smell pervaded the air.

Early next morning a couple of tall, kilted Scotsmen towered over my bunk as they gave me a tray of breakfast, hot and ample. 'Come on, laddie, get this doon and you'll feel a wee bit better,' one of them boomed. I was overwhelmed by their kindness and my one regret is that I never saw either of them again. My thoughts went back to the happy times I had known in Glasgow in my earliest years.

Within a day or two a signal came through ordering me to report to RAF Leuchars and then to proceed as best I could – which meant scrounging a lift – to RAF Sunburgh. It was my good fortune to find a pilot who was a jazz fan, a great admirer of Benny Goodman and Artie Shaw. When I told him that I too played the clarinet, he said he would be happy to help me if I could be ready in ten minutes.

My luck was certainly in, for the thought had already crossed my mind that no 'kite' was likely to be hanging around Leuchars just for the privilege of flying me to Sunburgh. I hastily paid my mess bill, packed my kit and ran to the waiting aircraft, an old Harrow stacked with vegetables. The rain came through the roof and there was no radio; but I was jolly thankful for the flight.

On arrival at Sunburgh my 'right-hand', Arthur Mouncey, and a couple of medical orderlies were there to greet me. I was given innoculations against typhoid and typhus, and the MO, 'Doc' Hendry, warned me to keep off the alcohol for a day or so.

On the first Sunday my five-piece band played in the Officers' Mess during the luncheon period. 'Doc' brought in drinks before we began playing and we knocked them back without needing his, 'Come on; these'll do you the world of good'. The effects were pretty bloody but we survived!

Within a month or so we had a new Commanding Officer, not a man with a wartime commission but a regular serving officer and a non-flying type. Our little band was playing out-of-camp gigs for 25 shillings a time each, the same rate as we had been getting at Wittering, although King's Regulations stipulated not more than five shillings out of pocket expenses. Within a few weeks the new CO found out what was going on and I was ordered to report to his office where he proceeded to 'wipe the floor' with me. 'This must not – repeat NOT – happen again, Sergeant,' he rapped out finally, somewhat to my dismay and that of the boys when I told them later that one of our perks was to be drastically reduced.

During War Weapons Week the band did some useful work in Lerwick, where it helped raise a considerable amount of money. Playing at dispersal points, where we provided the only entertainment for the aircrews, was another worthwhile job we did. We were also very much in demand by visiting stars who needed us to back them at camp concerts. I vividly recall the time when Gracie Fields came to Sunburgh to entertain the troops. As she came on stage Gracie spotted that the front rows were occupied only by officers. She immediately walked off and refused to return until the officers had given up their seats to the 'erks'. You can be sure that she received a great ovation that night!

Eggs were plentiful during my time in the Shetlands, so I sent a lot home to Tessa in our cottage at Easton-on-the-Hill. Having a free issue of cigarettes each week, I used the empty tins for packaging the eggs. But despite my careful packing I'm afraid that most of the eggs arrived not only smashed but accompanied by a strong flavour of tobacco. I don't know whether any of them were usable. I never asked!

While I was in the Shetlands I was shown over the ill-fated submarine *Shad*. The torpedoes were enormously long and almost touched the mess tables. The lack of space was even more acute than I had imagined: it appeared to be virtually impossible to move around in a hurry without banging into something. It was a rewarding experience and I would have liked to have repeated it. The submarine was based at Lerwick, about 28 miles from Sunburgh. We were driven over there by Sgt 'Ginger' Skinner, the NCO in charge of transport. The way he drove and the speed he took bends led me to think we were more likely to see the inside of a hospital than a submarine that day. I was not sure we would ever make it back to camp either, with 'Ginger' making so many detours to visit girl friends and collect eggs.

While I was stationed in the Shetlands I again became disenchanted with the music side of my RAF duties. As I had earlier, I felt I wanted to do something more positive in my service life, so I decided to concentrate on learning the Morse Code with a view to remustering to airfield control. However, my mind seemed exhausted: I was generally agitated and anxious and was unable to memorise beyond the letter 'H'. When I reported sick the MO prescribed bromide three times a day, which I took for most of the eight and a half months the band and I spent in the Shetlands before we were posted back to Central Band Headquarters.

A lot of dance band musicians had passed through Uxbridge since I was there in 1940, including many of my former Ambrose colleagues – Archie Craig, Eric Breeze, Tommy McQuater, Clinton Ffrench, George Chisholm, Harry Lewis, Andy McDevitt, Jimmy Miller, Jock Cummings and Sid Colin, all of whom became major figures in the No 1 RAF dance band, the famous Squadronaires. When my band and I reported to the less than friendly Orderly Room, we found that Cpl Steve Race, guitarist Howard Lucraft and Sgt Fred Bayco (an undistinguished pre-war cinema organist) were still working there. Having come from one of the 'far flung outposts', it was only natural for us to take the view that the office staff at Uxbridge were holding down some pretty soft jobs.

Within a few days of returning to Central Band HQ, I was given a medical examination which revealed that not only was I unfit for duty but also unfit for any further posting. The RAF despatched me to Mill Hill Military Hospital where I was prescribed benzadrine by day and phenobarbitone by night. I did not know, nor did I particularly care, what was happening to me until on 31 December 1943 I was medically discharged from the RAF as an anxiety neurosis case.

17 'Hello Again'

Back at our cottage in Easton I was slowly weaning myself off the drugs that had been pumped into me. One day in early January 1944 I received a letter (redirected from our London address) from Maurice Winnick inviting me to join a 'good band' he was forming at Ciro's Club. A day or so later, while I was still thinking it over, our landlady called in to say that a gentleman by the name of Geraldo was telephoning from London. Gerry, as he was called in the profession, offered me a place in his orchestra. I told him I had not been all that well and that I hadn't played for more than four months. He suggested that I didn't rush into any decision at once but should meet him at the BBC studios in the Aeolian Hall in Bond Street in three weeks time.

I thought over both these offers and then decided to go and see Gerry, at the same time making arrangements to move back to our London home in Brondesbury Road.

I arrived at the studio more in body than in mind: it wasn't the same as practising at home! The first band number had 16 bars *ad lib* tenor solo, and although the chords were there to guide me, I didn't think I had played too impressively. I got through the rehearsal with an effort. Afterwards drummer Maurice Burman put his arm round my shoulder and said, 'That was great, Billy; just like old times.' He was almost the only one to give me any encouragement and I was forever grateful to him for having helped me get back to normal.

On 30 January Gerry announced: 'We're going to include the Glenn Miller version of *Bugle Call Rag*.' This was the arrangement with the up tempo tenor solo that Glenn had recorded. At first Gerry relaxed the tempo for me and with some practice I managed to master it; then he gradually increased the pace up to that of the Miller recording, and as he did so I could sense that my playing was improving . . .

After one performance at the Palladium Maurice whispered in my ear, 'Aubrey Frank [my predecessor] used to go down front to play that solo.' So the following evening when we played *Bugle Call Rag* I stepped down from the foot high rostrum and walked forward nearly to the footlights. I noticed Gerry giving me a questioning look, but I chose to ignore him and played the solo. As I finished, much to my astonishment many in the audience applauded. My ego having received a suitable boost, I returned to my place, sat down and carried on playing as Maurice nodded approvingly. One evening at the end of yet another performance of that number, Burman quipped: 'It's a pity Aubrey Frank didn't go down front!' We both laughed heartily. Maurice Burman was one of the finest chaps I've had the pleasure of knowing, and as I have often said when remembering him – 'there was only one Churchill, one Ambrose, one Chaplin, and one Burman'.

When Glenn Miller and the USAAF band were in England during the latter part of 1944, we were playing at the Palladium once again, and Gerry thought it was appropriate to include in his programme the Miller favourite *My Guy's Come Back*, with the excellent Wally Stott arrangement. Following Sid Bright's piano introduction and the first chorus, the stage lights were dimmed so as to allow bassist Jack Collier and guitarist Ivor Mairants to go down front to do their spot in the number. As Ivor rested his leg on the chair and started to play, he realised he had no amplification. Someone had pulled the plug out of the amplifier! Taking a quick look back at me he hissed: 'Billy, Billy', as though I were to blame. They carried on playing with no one apparently noticing the lack of amplification – not even Gerry who stood with that stage smile on his face. After the concert a furious Ivor threatened to smash my instruments, but luckily Maurice Burman was able to calm him down. We later discovered that tenor man George Harris, who was not a fully-fledged 'lumberer', was the culprit.

I first saw and heard the Glenn Miller USAAF band 'live' when they broadcast from the Paris Cinema Studios in Lower Regent Street. When I arrived the place was packed, but that famous Miller reedman Michael 'Peanuts' Hucko took me in through the rear door. Glenn was having an argument with the BBC engineers about how many microphones he required for the broadcast. Happily the matter was soon resolved to his satisfaction and I was able to enjoy one of the greatest musical experiences of my life. The orchestra's performance became indelibly stamped on my mind as I listened to the marks of expression Miller employed. The playing of an *ff* passage followed immediately by a *pp* passage for four muted trombones provided an exciting contrast. And that was by no means all. I might have missed this musical treat altogether if the *Melody Maker* had been correct when reporting on their front page in November 1942 that Glenn Miller was to join the US Navy!

'Peanuts' Hucko and I became good friends and he gave me a Selmer HS Double Star clarinet mouthpiece which I used for many years. When I first met him and the Miller boys, they wanted to know where Ambrose was playing. Drummer Ray McKinley suggested we play some of 'Ammy's' recordings. Ray's own recording of *Tea for Two* appealed to me greatly, and so did the other side, *Basin Street Boogie*, which featured 'Peanuts'. Geraldo was kind enough to ask Arthur Berkby, one of his staff arrangers, to write out the score from the record. I have played that arrangement many times over the radio.

When both the Geraldo and the Miller bands were in London, some of us – including Glenn – would rendezvous after work at the Knightsbridge apartment of Lady Ulick Brown, Maurice Burman's sister Alma. There we would have a few drinks, listen to records, and have a blow ourselves. I would play tenor while 'Peanuts' played clarinet, then we would swap over, he going onto tenor and I onto clarinet. I am a keen collector of badges and one night at the flat Glenn, noticing my interest, pulled one from his tunic pocket and asked, 'How'd ya like to have this one?' It was a metal badge faced with the Stars and Stripes in enamel: I kept it for nearly 40 years. Although Glenn had a reputation as something of a disciplinarian, many of his musicians paid little regard to his military rank. Some of the boys in the band told me that Miller's pianist/arranger Mel Powell would sometimes read the *Daily Worker* at rehearsals, just to 'needle' that rather Right-wing Major!

When Glenn Miller was in England he would invite British artists to appear in his radio broadcasts. There came a day when Len Camber, one of Gerry's vocalists, received a telephone call with an invitation from Glenn to do a 'guest' spot on Miller's next radio show. Len accepted with alacrity. Trombonist Jock Bain and I were in Maurice Burman's flat when Len burst in to tell us the news. His date was for the following Tuesday at the Paris Cinema Studios. However, on the Monday Len had a further 'phone call to say that the date had been postponed indefinitely. He was too embarrassed to tell his friends, though we all knew about it because it was Maurice who had impersonated Miller. Len never did find out who it was; but I don't think he was too disappointed – another couple of Geraldo concerts and his female fans were crowding the stage door for him!

The two top bands in 1944 were, according to the *Melody Maker* annual poll, the Squadronaires and Geraldo's. This rating was reflected in the tremendous ovation given the Geraldo band by the lads in the Services when we were invited to open the new NAAFI in Lincoln. Staying there overnight in a hotel I remembered the Bracebridge Military Hospital where I had spent a short time the previous year. But when I asked the young lady receptionist how far away it was and mentioned that I had once been a patient there, she recoiled slightly. I then realised she must have known that Bracebridge used to be a lunatic asylum!

On tour a few of us would hold 'bandroom jam sessions', just for the fun of it. Maurice Burman switched from drums to cornet; Douggie Robinson and I competed on clarinet in a style Maurice described as 'whorehouse jazz', played mainly in the lower register, with trumpeter Freddy Clayton and Jock Bain on trombone. Popular singer Johnny Green took over on drums and proved to be the best 'suitcase drummer' we had ever heard.

In what free time there was I was able to fit in a radio series – 'Navy Mixture' – for Charles Shadwell, broadcasting alternatively from Portsmouth and Southampton. That over, I took a short holiday with Tessa revisiting Easton-on-the-Hill. It was a strange feeling to drive past my old RAF camp at Wittering as a 'civvie'. Nearing the local bus stop I spotted a familiar face – former Station Warrant Officer Culf, also in 'civvies'. I stopped to tell him where we were going and to ask him what he was doing now he was out of the 'mob'. 'Going to Easton!' he replied. 'I always thought you were a bit weird. Me? I'm a waiter in the Officers' Mess.' I found it a bit hard to suppress a laugh for he had once told me that he wanted to be a commissionaire when his Service days were over. I could have just imagined him as that, swaggering around in a flash uniform; but not as a waiter. Some years later, on another visit to Easton, I called at my old RAF camp and told the 'erk' on duty at the gate that I was Sergeant in charge of the band there during the war. He was not impressed, simply replying, 'Big deal!'

In the late summer of 1944 Geraldo and his Orchestra played a number of Forces concerts at the Queensbury Club followed by a further appearance at a Jazz Jamboree in October. Our 15-piece lineup at this time comprised: Alfie Noakes, Tim Casey, Chick Smith (t); Ted Heath, Eric Tann, Joe Ferrie (tb); Wally Stott, Douggie Robinson, George Harris and myself (saxes); Phil Goody (fl & bar); Sid Bright (p); Maurice Burman (d); Ivor Mairants (g); Jack Collier (bs); plus vocalists Len Camber and Johnny Green.

Early in November Field Marshall Montgomery requested Geraldo to make a tour of France, Belgium and Holland to play for the Forces. We were soon on our way.

18   With Geraldo on a Wartime Tour in Europe

We started a 17-day tour, sailing from Newhaven to Dieppe on 13 November, after making a cautious approach to the French port which had not yet been completely cleared of enemy mines. As we left Dieppe we saw the V1s flying high across the Channel, and when we heard that they were falling on London our thoughts naturally turned to the folks at home and our concern for their safety.

It was a precarious journey to Paris, for the roads had also not yet been made safe from German mines. We travelled in six trucks under orders to stay in convoy with no unscheduled stops. I was in the last truck along with Len Camber and Maurice Burman, and we made at least two unauthorised stops on account of Maurice's weak bladder. This made Maurice somewhat unpopular with the rest of the convoy who were obliged to halt each time. The trucks, which also contained our instruments and props, turned out to be not only uncomfortable but very cold at this time of the year. Some of the boys bitched a little about this, although Phil Goody and I seemed to care rather less. As the only ex-servicemen in the party we were used to some pretty basic forms of transport.

On 15 November we played the first of six gala performances in Paris at the ENSA Garrison Theatre – the Théâtre de Marigny on the Champs-Elysées – for the show *Gay Salute*, which starred Noël Coward and included Frances Day, Nervo and Knox, Will Hay & Co, and Bobby Howes. However, so far as the lads in uniform were concerned, Geraldo's band was the highspot of the night.

Before leaving France we played for SHAEF in the little Antoinette theatre at Versailles.

While we were in Paris Ted Heath thought he had a sharp eye for business. One day he disappeared down a side street with his suitcase filled with cigarettes, soap, tea and coffee – all goods in short supply. Later he returned with the most fashionable Parisian style in fur coats – but what a shame they were made from cats' furs! Throughout the London bombings Ted, who was over military age, used to carry that suitcase of his on frequent visits to Maurice Burman's flat at the White House, Regents Park, where Aubrey Frank, bassist Tommy Bromley and Johnny Green also lived. They were all intrigued to know why he did so and eventually asked Ted straight out: he replied, 'I'll show you if you'll keep it to yourselves.' Opening the suitcase he revealed that it was full of paper money. They say you can't take it with you but Ted must have thought that if the Nazis were going to blow his money up he might as well be with it!

The day before we left Paris for Brussels I was astonished to receive a 'phone call from Jacques, a saxophonist I had met with Ambrose in Cannes in 1937. After a cordial greeting he said he had many *anches* (reeds) for me. These were made in Paris by Vandoren, though they were extremely difficult to find in wartime. I was more than pleased to make an appointment to meet him at midday at his apartment, which was not far from our hotel. Maurice Burman, Ivor Mairants and I then took a stroll during which we observed how popular music was being 'plugged' in Paris near the end of the war. A small group of musicians was playing on a street corner accompanying a singer while two other fellows offered the sheet music for sale to passers-by – which was certainly one way of conducting business.

As mid-day approached I asked my two companions, whose knowledge of French was undoubtedly better than mine, to ask the way to Jacques' address. I felt a trifle let down when they said they were off to their room to rest before rehearsal. I sauntered off alone and after showing the address to several people I finally found the right block. I asked a woman sitting at a desk in the hall for Jacques' apartment and she went away without indicating whether or not she had understood my less than fluent French. After a few minutes she returned with a seedy-looking fellow who might have been the janitor but certainly wasn't Jacques. In the meantime I had noticed a steady procession of men passing up and down the stairway, some of them looking furtively over their shoulders. At last I realised that I was in a brothel and had been 'lumbered' again. But by whom?

Back in my hotel room the 'phone rang, and . . . 'Billee, I didn't see you; what happened? . . .' I dropped the 'phone and dashed into the adjoining room just in time to catch Maurice Burman on the other end of the line talking about '*anches*' . . .

Maurice was a great organiser, especially of social events. Having found out that a number of RAF aircrew types were having a party in a private house and would appreciate a little jazz, he secured an invitation for the 'jazzers' – Douggie Robinson, Jack Collier, Freddy Clayton, Len Camber and I. Naturally, it turned out to be a gargantuan drinking session with the boys jazzing it up far into the night. We were breaking curfew but the RAF lads took us across Brussels to our hotel by Jeep before dawn, each of us clutching a present of a bottle of spirits. As we returned to our rooms someone suggested bidding a late goodnight – or early good morning – to Julie Dawn, one of our girl singers; so we staggered into her room and, sprawling over her bed, bored her (I suspect) with the story of the night's frivolities. In later years Julie developed into a charming radio personality with her own slot on Radio 2's 'You and the Night and the Music'; and she still sings beautifully.

At the end of our first concert in Brussels Field Marshall Bernard Montgomery came backstage to thank us. He told us that he had heard the Geraldo orchestra many times and now he had the pleasure of meeting it as the first unit of its kind to entertain the troops in the European theatre of war. When he came up to shake each one of us by the hand, I automatically stood to attention when he came to me!

In Brussels the ENSA mail was collected from the third floor of a building which only a short while before had been the Gestapo headquarters. I had occasion to visit the mail room where there was a wall map still in place and showing with red-topped pins the sitings of all the V1s that had fallen on London. It gave the impression that our capital city had been wiped out – so much for the accuracy of the indicators! In the basement of the building was the Gestapo 'interrogation room' . . .

A lot of Belgians in the music business came to hear the band play while we were in Brussels, and it was thus that I met Johnny Kleuger, brother of a prominent music publisher. Being Jewish he had been rounded up by the Germans and sent to a concentration camp outside the city. He told me about the ghastly treatment inflicted on the inmates. One example was the way unfortunates were forced to jump into a trench some ten feet deep carrying full packs; then they had to climb out again by ladder and repeat the procedure again and again until they collapsed exhausted. Johnny was lucky to escape: working on the roads out of camp, he got away in a car with the help of two non-Jewish patriot friends who up until then had avoided the Nazi clutches.

One evening Johnny introduced me to a pretty blonde, a former member of the Belgian underground who during the Occupation had rarely slept in the same bed on two consecutive nights in order to avoid being picked up by the Gestapo. At the Brussels theatre where we were working, one of the electricians was unable to stand up straight, having been kicked in the testicles with exceptional violence by Nazi thugs.

One pleasant morning in Brussels a few of us took a stroll along a street that until the early 1940s had been predominantly Jewish. We drifted into a wine shop where the proprietor told us in halting English how he had managed to harbour a Jewish couple during the years of occupation. As he finished telling us the actual couple came into the shop and confirmed the truth of all he had told us.

Moving on into Holland we played at the Philips Theatre in Eindhoven, and who should be there in the audience but Sgt 'Ginger' Skinner from my RAF days in the Shetlands – and he immediately recognised me. Backstage, I introduced him to the boys and to our girl singers, Julie Dawn and Sally Douglas, after which Ted Heath suggested that we invite Ginger back to our room for a noggin. (Ted knew that I usually carried a bottle of Scotch on tour.) We finished the bottle in quick time, for Ginger was a sergeant with a lot of practice and we were not far behind! Ted promised to replace the Scotch, and true to his word brought me a bottle the next day. I thought what a decent chap he was until one evening I took a nip only to find I was drinking cold tea! Ted of course was another of the 'lumberers'. A few years later when he was leading his own famous band, his coach driver was . . . 'Ginger' Skinner.

We met up with BBC war correspondent Franklin Engelman in Eindhoven. His Jeep stacked with recording gear, he was as always chasing the action. I met him again several years later in rather different circumstances: he was on the dance floor of the Savoy Hotel and I was fronting the band. I reminded him that the last time we had met, it was gunfire not music we could hear.

Although there was no shortage of food in the ENSA hostel there were plenty of hungry kids outside. This prompted us to take them something to eat when we could; and at Douggie Robinson's suggestion we gave the older men all the cigarettes and tobacco we could spare as they seemed desperate for a smoke.

On the playing side I remember that we performed in some very poorly lit concert halls, especially in Tilberg, a town where most of the electricity generators had been destroyed by the retreating Germans.

Before leaving for home on 30 November we were shown round the famous Philips factory where I purchased three electric razors, which were quite a novelty in those days. When we flew into Northolt I declared a bottle of Champagne and the three razors to a Customs Officer who thought the razors must be liable for duty but could find no reference to such newfangled gadgets in his regulations, so he let me pass uncharged.

Soon after our return to England, Maurice Burman asked me to do a gig at the USAAF camp in Cambridge on New Year's Eve. One did not refuse Maurice, and although I remember being driven to the base I recall little of the journey home, except that it was a crazy drive by Jeep. Jack Collier, who played alongside me, was my drinking partner for the night, during which we must have blown *Deep in the Heart of Texas* a dozen times or more.

19 'Gerry'

I remember Carmen Mastrem, Glenn Miller's guitarist, once saying exactly what I felt – that after playing in a small group for a while the novelty wears off and one longs to be part of a big band. Then after a spell with a big band one yearns for the small group again! It was happening to me now and Geraldo, sensing that I felt unsettled, called me to his office in Bond Street. When I explained the situation to him, he was understanding and promised to arrange for me to have a band within his band. He was as good as his word and supplied a lineup similar to that of Ambrose's Embassy Eight of ten years before: Freddy Clayton (t); Jock Bain (tb); George Harris and myself (reeds); Sid Bright (p); Ivor Mairants (g); Jack Collier (b); and Maurice Burman (d). It was this grouping that inspired me to compose and arrange for small jazz combos. Many of my orchestrations have been published by the Peter Maurice Co and other music publishers. I have always felt grateful to Gerry who treated me well both as a musician and as a person.

Geraldo, born Gerald Bright and a youthful piano prodigy, received a classical education at the Royal Academy of Music and in 1940 had been appointed Director of Dance Music at the BBC. He was a conductor of considerable skill who once excelled himself in the Royal Albert Hall when he conducted the massed forces of the BBC Symphony Orchestra, the RAF Orchestra, the Geraldo Orchestra and the Choir. He was as solid as a rock. It all seemed a far cry from the days when I first knew of him – in 1930 – as a tall handsome figure with glossy black hair and a neat moustache, colourfully dressed in the imagined Gaucho style as he led his Tango Orchestra at the Savoy Hotel. *Lady of Spain* was his signature tune then, long before he adopted *Hello Again*.

Gerry had his funny side too. He was a Cockney, as I am, and he spoke like one all his life. The more mature ladies who patronised the Savoy were often clearly inclined towards him. One of them once insisted on him having the use of her Rolls Royce and chauffeur for a couple of weeks. The chauffeur had what used to be called an 'Oxford accent' and I used to joke that at the end of the fortnight Gerry had an 'Oxford' accent and the chauffeur spoke like a Cockney. Gerry made one of his classic announcements at the close of our 'Music Shop' radio programmes: 'Ladies and gen'leman, we've come ter the end of the programme, the clock on the wall says 'alf pass ten, so we're gonna shut up the shop and pull dahn the shutters.' Another time he announced, 'We've just played a British 'it and now we're going to play a French 'it.' I'm afraid it didn't sound quite the way he meant it! I coined a phrase, 'the Geraldo School of Elocution'. He took it in good part, but I was always mystified by his manner of speech because none of his family that I knew, including his twin brother Sid, spoke that way.

I spent 21 months with Geraldo in a band which was acknowledged as being the best British dance orchestra of the 1940s. During the war most British dance bands went into a decline due to the drafting of many of their key players into the Armed Forces. It says much for Geraldo's judgment that he invariably brought in top class replacements and so enabled his band to be regarded as the British equivalent of Glenn Miller's. The high standard maintained by Geraldo was due in no small part to the work of his arrangers, notably Wally Stott, whose arrangement of *Laura* was an outstanding example.

We went out on a variety tour of the country in 1945 and while we were in Newcastle, playing at the Empire in June, Ted Heath left to form his own big band which he led so successfully for the better part of 25 years. I did not know it at the time, but I too would be leaving within three months. Walking through Regents Park one afternoon in late August I chanced to meet Ambrose who told me that he would be taking a band back into Ciro's Club within a month, and he asked me to rejoin him along with some of the other 'old boys', including Max Goldberg and Les Carew. I thought the matter over and decided to accept. The following day at the EMI studios I intimated to Geraldo that I wished to hand in my notice. 'I discuss business only in my office,' he replied tersely. I already knew that he would not be overjoyed, for if anyone was giving notice he liked to be the one to give it. Next day I went to his office, where he offered me a cigar (although the boys never did believe me!) as I stated my reasons for wanting to leave. 'Why don't you think it over?' Gerry suggested, then: 'Aren't you happy with me?' I told him that I was but simply had this urge to rejoin Ambrose with whom I had spent nine enjoyable years. In my view the Ambrose orchestra had been the best of all bands and I sincerely hoped (and believed) that it would be so again.

20 'When Day is Done'

When Ambrose and his Orchestra returned to Ciro's Club on the evening of 8 October 1945, after an absence of more than eight years, they were accorded a most handsome reception by both clientèle and staff. Captain Nathan, the manager, made us very welcome while Louis, the headwaiter, bowed almost to the floor as he greeted 'Ammy'! Among the well-known names that night and later were Prince Aly Khan, Harry Roy's wife, daughter of the white Raja of Sarawak and known as 'Princess Pearl', and members of the Rafael Tuck and the Marks and Spencer families, and Geraldo and his wife. Sometimes 'Princess Pearl' was accompanied by her sister Baba and Harry Roy's sister, who we rather wickedly nicknamed 'Princess Becky'! When Prince Aly Khan took the dance floor with Rita Hayworth towards the end of the evening the management usually dimmed the lights so as to afford them an intimate atmosphere.

Our lineup was: Max Goldberg, Leslie 'Jiver' Hutchinson (t); Les Carew (tb); Harry Smith, Nat Temple (as); Johnny Gray and myself (ts); Malcolm Lockyer (p); Tommy Bromley (b); Alan Metcalfe (g); Norman Burns (d); Sid Simone (vln and dep. ldr.). My salary at that time was £25 a week plus £2.6s for a broadcast from the Club and £6.5s for a broadcast from the BBC studios; and I was paid £4 for a recording session.

It was not long after returning to Ciro's that Ambrose decided to engage a second trombone. I suggested Abe Walters and Ambrose asked him to audition by sitting in with the band one night until we finished. Soon after 2am, when all the customers had gone home, Abe turned to me enquiringly. I looked up at 'Ammy' who was sitting in the balcony with Captain Nathan, and almost whispered: 'Does he get the job?' 'Is he comfortable, Billy?' Ambrose replied. 'Yes, Bert, he's very comfortable,' I said. 'Well then, let him stay and be comfortable,' 'Ammy' responded with a shrug of a shoulder. Within two years Abe Walters was himself to become a bandleader at the Embassy Club, Ciro's Club and then the exclusive Nightingale Club where he led a seven-piece outfit in the then popular Latin–American style. I had kidded him into wearing a white dinner jacket and sporting a toothbrush moustache, but as he was leading a rhumba band and calling hiself 'Don Carlos' it seemed quite appropriate! From the easy-going chap I had known with Ambrose he became a hard guy to work for, as I discovered on the odd occasions I played for him. On the first night he called me aside and asked me not to address him as Abe. 'My name is now Don,' he said pointedly. His front line consisted of only one trumpet and a flute doubling clarinet; Abe – or rather 'Don' – led on piano with the addition of guitar, drums, bass and maracas – and what a popular recording band it was!

During the engagement at Ciro's Rudy Vallee visited England once again. The former sax player in the Savoy Havana Band of 1924/5 who was never allowed to sing with that outfit but had become a singing idol in his own country, had been signed to take part in the cabaret at Ciro's, as the 'star'. This well-groomed chap with a charming personality and pleasant if somewhat nasal singing voice, was puzzled when singing his own arrangement of *It Ain't Necessarily So* with a special ending of 'It Ain't Nece . . . It Ain't Nece . . . It Ain't Necessarily So' . . . to hear the band whispering in the background, 'It Ain't Tessa . . . It Ain't Tessa . . . It Ain't Tessa-ssarily So! He was highly amused when it was explained to him that Tessa was my wife.

I remember too that he had Lord Louis Mountbatten, Sir Malcolm Sargent and their wives spellbound with his *All Points West* number.

As he danced around at Ciro's Club Sir Malcolm Sargent invariably had a smile and a nod for the saxophone section seated in the front line of the band.

I must confess that I didn't appreciate playing from 9pm until 2am once again, nor playing choruses of the sentimental and banal tunes of the period for most of the night. We had more than a normal complement for a West End club band, so we played *pianissimo* until the last hour or so when we would feature our special arrangements, which were something between the pre-war style and radio scores. They were enjoyable enough for a club, but I was missing the fully-blown radio arrangements. Matters improved when we began regular weekly broadcasts, with Anne Shelton and Ray Burns making a fine vocal team. Arthur Mouncey (my 'right-hand' at RAF Wittering) was added to the trumpet section and Alan Dean was engaged as additional singer.

Alan, who was later to be signed up by the American General Artists Corporation, made a name for himself at Ciro's, but I didn't make it easy for him. One night Alan stepped forward to the microphone and as he started to sing, 'Ammy' turned round to the band, and speaking to no one in particular as usual, muttered, 'Why must he have his hand held to his throat?' Alan kept his hand up there for an hour or more until the interval. Then I returned his bow tie and he my tenor cap!

On 8 March 1946 we were invited for a second time to play at Buckingham Palace. I remember being paid £10 for the date. I had instructions from Tessa to memorise the dresses worn by the Queen and the two Princesses, as well as their hair styles. Being blessed with a photographic memory I did not find those orders too difficult to carry out! Tessa's special interest arose because she had been a top model for hair stylists Xavier of Knightsbridge, Barry Woolf of Piccadilly and the famous Eugène. The Queen enjoyed her favourite Viennese waltz, while the young Princesses enthusiastically requested the 'Boogie Woogie' which was all the rage in the mid-1940s.

While we were fulfilling this Royal engagement, the management at Ciro's had table cards printed for their patrons –

Ciro's closed for a couple of summer months and Ambrose took the band to Monte Carlo for a seasonal engagement, leaving on 18 July. With Tessa and Joe Crossman – who replaced Harry Smith – we set off in my car, travelling by way of Newhaven–Dieppe–Paris. Between Paris and Monte Carlo I was taken ill on an overnight stop and admitted to hospital with food poisoning! I was in considerable pain when they gave me an injection – and as I drifted into unconsciousness I dimly saw and heard Bill Lewington ask where my petrol coupons were . . . I hoped he was joking! In the early hours of the morning as the effects of the injection wore off, I was aware of two Sisters of Mercy standing over me, whispering in French – and for a few moments I really thought my end was nigh! However, I made a quick recovery and having thanked nurse Arse (yes; that was her name) we were once more on our way to Monto Carlo.

The day after our arrival we rehearsed at the New Beach Casino and met the other band who were playing opposite us – a five piece combination led by French jazz guitarist Marcel Bianci. They all doubled and would often feature three violins, although at other times they sounded like Artie Shaw's Gramercy Five. We never tired of listening to them. Music of a different kind was provided in the large square opposite where the symphony orchestra gave concerts. I became friendly with one of the viola players whose wife hailed from Bradford. They invited Tessa and I to a broadcast at the Monte Carlo radio station where we were amused to see the orchestra's lady harpist doing her knitting during a tacit period . . . not an uncommon sight in some parts of the world! About eight of us listened to the broadcast in a separate room where Tessa and I had an 'embarrassing experience' – as the late Wilfred Pickles used to say. A mosquito settled on the thigh of a lady wearing shorts. I slapped it – or rather her thigh – and the next few seconds were mildly awkward! However, following my apology, in schoolroom French, she laughed and the situation was eased.

We passed a delightful five weeks in Monte Carlo, except for the time when Tessa went down with sunstroke after I had taken her out on the 'Med' in a pedallo. After that she stayed out of the sun and played the gaming tables; I joined her there when I was free, although one was not supposed to play the tables if one was working in the place. I would stroll in wearing a dinner jacket and smoking a cigar and trying not to look like a 'worker'. Les Carew and Joe Crossman, the fitness fanatics, spent most of their leisure time playing tennis, while Aubrey Frank, who had come in place of Johnny Gray and had told me before we left England that he would return home if the trip was not to his liking, showed no signs of leaving. One week Ambrose took the unusual course of paying us on the beach. He was in a hurry when I met him there by chance, and handing me a large brown envelope full of paper money, he asked me to 'be a good boy and pay the fellows for me and give Joe Crossman an extra 1000 francs for helping us out.' Joe was amused by that: he had only come to Monte Carlo for the fun of it anyway!

The engagement over, Tessa and I stayed on for a few days before motoring to Paris for a week's holiday. It was not by coincidence that we saw and heard Stephane Grappelli and Django Reinhardt while we were there.

We re-opened at Ciro's on 18 September and not long afterwards our bassist Tommy Bromley had to leave on medical grounds, having been advised by his doctor to take a rest from the long hours of work. Tommy and his attractive wife Bobbie returned to Monte Carlo which they had so much enjoyed during the summer. Sadly, we learned later that Tommy had died as the result of a motor accident when his car went off the road, over a cliff and into the sea between Cannes and Monte Carlo. In March 1941 Tommy had suffered leg injuries in the bombing of the Café de Paris in London which killed his leader Ken 'Snakehips' Johnson and tenor saxist Dave Williams.

Ambrose's engagement at Ciro's Club came to an abrupt end on 19 March 1947. This was near the end of the winter of the Big Freeze when the music business in London's West End was severely hit by the weather. As we were on the bandstand ready to play to an empty room, Ambrose walked in looking downcast and spotting Captain Nathan at his table in the balcony, joined him. In the silence of the room we heard 'Ammy' say, 'You don't need us here, Nathan, do you?' 'Not really,' came the reply.

And so we finished. The dance band days as I had known them for the previous 20 years had finished also, though I may not have realised it at the time. It was the end of a golden era; The Golden Age Of The Dance Bands, as it has so often been called.

'I Miss You Most Of All When Day Is Done' . . .

21 Freelancing

For two years in 1946 and 1947 I served on the London District Committee of the Musicians' Union. I was proposed from the floor to organise the band for the May Day march in both years because I had the experience of leading a band on the march from my RAF days. In 1946 the effort was entirely voluntary in that all the fellows gave their time and energy for no payment. Many well-known musicians took part, including Tony Thorpe, Van Phillips, Maurice Burman, Bill Lewington, Arthur Mouncey, Harry and Laurie Gold, Max Goldberg and Ivor Mairants. In 1947 the band was fully paid at Union rates, although others were free to join in if they so wished.

Serving on the Committee entailed my attending meetings at 10am, and as I did not finish work for Ambrose at Ciro's Club until 2am, I found my commitment to the Union somewhat exhausting at times. Moreover, I was also serving on a Sub-Committee. At the end of two years it was apparent that the Union activity was having an adverse effect on my work as a musician; so I regretfully resigned from the London District Committee. However, I left knowing that I had been instrumental in obtaining a fair wage for some of the bands. One example was the Covent Garden Orchestra, for whose members we secured a weekly wage of £20.

The Musician's Social and Benevolent Council has always been a credit to the Musician's Union. I cannot detail here all the excellent work done by the various organisers, but I would like to pay special tribute to Harry Flaum who, since he started work on behalf of the MSBC in 1941 has collected more than £170,000 and at the age of nearly 90 continues to act as collector. It was the MSBC which sponsored the 'Jazz Jamboree' which in 1944 featured the American AEF band conducted by Glenn Miller.

Apart from my work for the Musicians' Union, I had a number of notable dates in my diary in addition to my job at Ciro's. I was so busy in fact that when the end at Ciro's came, I didn't really notice the loss. Before that happened, however, on the second Sunday in November 1946, I played in pianist/vocalist Hamish Menzies' four-piece band which opened the Rose Room Sunday Club at Chez Auguste in Soho. Ivor Mairants was on guitar and Jack Fallon on bass. Many bandleaders were there for the opening, including Ted Heath, George Shearing, Reg Leopold, Nat Temple, Percival Mackey, George Melachrino, Harry Gold and Chappie D'Amato. Ambrose and Geraldo were in New York at the time, both making statements to the effect that British musicians in general were lazy and had little incentive to create and were wasting their time and talents by imitation and copying American records and arrangements. These remarks brought swift reactions from Ted Heath and Teddy Thorne (of Cyril Stapleton's band) in defence of the British dance band musician.

Early in 1947 I appeared with the London Symphony Orchestra at the Royal Albert Hall to play the tenor saxophone solo in Ravel's *Bolero*, Walter Goehr conducting. I sat through the programme for about 45 minutes before we reached *Bolero*, the suspense making me very apprehensive. The theme is played by a multitude of instruments, of course, and when the clarinettist, a small fat fellow, began his solo with a 'squeak' I felt some relief, for he had made a human error and experienced reed trouble, something that most clarinet players suffer at one time or another. The really difficult part, so far as I am concerned, is the counting of bars while waiting for one's entry. Having played the tenor solo to my satisfaction, I settled down for some 15 to 20 minutes for my solo in Prokofiev's *Lieutenant Kijé* Suite, counting with the utmost concentration, which I strongly advise since the conductor attempted to bring me in eight bars too soon. I confidently ignored him, continued to count and came in correctly!

In the middle of March I celebrated 21 years in the music business by blossoming out as a bandleader on radio when I began recording a series of programmes entitled 'The Amstell Way', again for ORBS. The programmes were 30 minutes long, and in the 'opener' I included ten of my own compositions, all exploiting four-beat jazz in a two-beat style, played by Leo Wright (t); Don Macaffer (tb); Alfie Kahn (ts); Malcolm Lockyer (p); Alan Metcalfe (g); Norman Burns (d); Ronnie Peters (b) with myself on clarinet. I was still a member of the Ambrose Orchestra, so my bandleading exploits at that time had to be confined to broadcasting and just the occasional public appearance.

On 30 March, the day after I had finished at Ciro's Club, I played another of our many Rose Room dates with my Quintette at the Chez Auguste. After we had played *How High the Moon* that jocular alto player Harry Conn asked for a tango! In later years Harry once quipped irreverently that Maurice Winnick's hearse driver had been caught for speeding.

The Rose Room Sunday night gigs were really a rendezvous for musicians, their wives, and music critics; I always thought of playing there as something of a challenge, although Danny Polo's clarinet, which he had given me, was beginning to play by itself. Eventually the club ran into financial difficulties and Sid Phillips bought it out, insisting that I continue there with my group. Sid and I were pretty close, so much so that at one time he asked me to become his manager; but I had to decline as I enjoyed playing more than anything (I still do!) and would not give it up for anyone.

My days were very full – recording with Ambrose on an average once a week; playing radio and TV dates with Louis Levy; deputising in Stanley Black's BBC orchestra, and judging some band contests. The latter were organised by the *Melody Maker* and I was invited onto the panel by critic Edgar Jackson.

On 6 July my Trio (Malcolm Lockyer, Norman Burns and myself) played one of our Rose Room Club gigs at the late Freddie Mills' restaurant – the last one at his place. Our genial host and compère that night was David Miller, who had announced the broadcasts from the London Casino during my days there with Jack Harris.

After this Tessa and I went on a three weeks holiday. We crossed from Dover to Boulogne and motored down to Monte Carlo for some swimming, sun bathing and wining and dining, not to mention a bit of gambling at the San Remo Casino, where they short changed us! We also paid a visit to Eze where some of the locals still lived in caves allowing their animals to wander in and out at will. At La Turbie we saw the ruins of a tower which is believed to have been built around 250 BC. I was taking a strictly non-working holiday, and after my previous visits to the South of France I found it strange (though hardly unwelcome) not to have to get dressed for work in the evenings.

Within a week of returning home I began a five week engagement with Nat Allen's band at Ciro's Club, from where we broadcast on Saturday nights, reminding me of the old Ambrosian times . . . With Nat I did a few TV transmissions from Alexandra Palace, where the ever busy little bandleader would dash off the set to change into a working-jacket around which he strapped his piano-accordion. He looked so creased, crumpled and uncomfortable that I was reminded of the film actor Lon Chaney who suffered much discomfort when adopting his elaborate disguises in macabre screen rôles. I must say that the job with Nat paid well enough – £21 a week plus an extra £3 for a broadcast from the club and £4 for a TV transmission. Furthermore, Nat never failed to feature me playing one of my own compositions.

I continued recording my ORBS programmes – from the Boosey & Hawkes studios in Regent Street – with Alan Dean singing, and 'The Amstell Way' hosted by a young fellow just out of the Navy, with an 'Oxford' accent – David Jacobs, who speaks even more 'posh' these days!

On some of my dates as 'deputy' in Stanley Black's BBC orchestra in 1947 I had the rewarding musical experience of playing alongside clarinet virtuoso and former child prodigy Willie Walker, and also with Bill Glover, formerly flautist with the Liverpool Philharmonic Orchestra. On one broadcast we featured Bill's arrangement of the samba *Cavaquinho*, and the very fast tempo at which it was played nearly knocked Stanley Black off his rostrum! Despite the terrific tempo every note was tongued, both Willie and Bill appeared to perform quite effortlessly. On a later date with Stanley Black at the BBC the famous classical clarinettist Jack Brymer gave a wonderful rendering of Victor Herbert's *Indian Summer* in which he not so much gave a technical performance as provided a study in tonal beauty.

Playing alongside so-called 'long hairs' I learned a lot, as I did indeed when sitting in with former child prodigy, clarinettist Frank Johnson (at one time a member of Jack Payne's Hotel Cecil Orchestra), fellow clarinettist Ted Shipway, flautist Jack Ellory and the other classical musicians.

22   BBC Calling

I took up a permanent position in Stanley Black's orchestra at the BBC on 5 October 1947, replacing Moss Kay, a fine multi-instrumentalist for whom I had deputised on occasions. It was his bad luck to be spotted playing in Maurice Winnick's band at Ciro's Club when he was taking a three weeks' paid holiday from the BBC. Mrs Tawny Neilson, one of the departmental heads at the BBC took a less than charitable view of his activity.

I have known Stanley Black for many, many years; in fact, together with saxophonist Harry Smith we used to go horse riding in Chingford as far back as 1931. I believe I was responsible for Stanley making his first arrangement for Ambrose in 1932; he had made a lovely version of *I Ain't Got No-body* (with one of Nat Gonella's very best vocals) in early 1931 at Levy's Oriole studios in Regent Street, and it was this that prompted me to suggest him to Ambrose. These days we know Stanley Black as an established conductor, the composer of numerous film scores and the holder of several Gold Discs for his Decca recordings; but in his youth he was a keen jazz player and orchestrator for a number of pre-war dance bands. I think that his scoring of Latin–American music – a taste for which he acquired when touring South America as a member of the Harry Roy band – has yet to be bettered. He is also a remarkable pianist with a brilliant technique, notwithstanding the fact that he has small hands and has seldom had time to practice. Geraldo was a fine conductor but Stanley Black was even better, so clear and distinct and a master over a wide field of music. The usual three hour rehearsal for a band broadcast was never exceeded; but it was not the same when he was indisposed and Charles Shadwell, a popular, kind and lovable man, though not in Stanley's class as a conductor, took over the baton.

The orchestra was a mixture of so-called 'jazzers' and 'long hairs' – all nice enough fellows although there were certainly no 'lumberers' among them, for the BBC frowned on any such frivolous behaviour.* When it was time to take a break, the 'gipsies' (most of them) would start playing cards while the brass section would pay a visit to the pub round the corner. The reed section, however, appeared to contain neither gamblers nor alcoholics! If he fancied a salt-beef sandwich during a

---

*The sax section comprised: Harry Hunter (lead as/cl); Bill Glover (lead fl/2nd as/cl); Manny Winters (lead cl/ts/fl); and myself as lead ts/cl. Each one of us was designated a lead player so that we could all be paid the same salary: only the BBC could have devised a scheme like that! At the end of my first broadcast with the orchestra from the Cripplegate Studios (where the Barbican Centre now stands) Stanley complimented me, saying, 'That's the best the saxes have ever sounded.'

long break, Stanley would give me a nod and we would meet upstairs to dash off to Kahns or the Nosh Bar in Windmill Street, where Bernard Delfont was a regular visitor. Another 'regular' to our band calls was David Land, a close friend of Stanley Black who completed the solo whist school of Bert Bullimore, Bill Glover and Les Maddox. David Land had the Dagenham Girl Pipers under contract and I think this must have been the prelude to his becoming connnected with show business. In later years he was of course to become the presenter of the stage musicals *Evita* and *Cats* in association with Robert Stigwood.

My first radio show with the orchestra took place at the Aeolian Hall where we backed Carol Levis, who introduced his 'discoveries' before an invited audience. During the recording of the programme poor Carol began rambling as his thoughts slipped back to the war years and he departed from the script, calling out – 'we won't let you down . . . we'll send food parcels . . . we will win . . .' He was led from the stage in front of a bewildered audience and after hurried consultations the recording was abandoned. Carol had been carrying far too much weight and it seems that as a result of suddenly going on too strict a diet his mind had become unbalanced. I heard later that some of his friends arranged to have him flown home to his native Canada where happily he made a rapid recovery.

The Stanley Black Orchestra backed some highly popular light comedy radio series including 'The Goon Show', the 'Bernard Braden Show', 'Life With the Lyons', 'Much Binding in the Marsh', 'Ray's a Laugh' and 'Up the Pole'. Then there was the regular Sunday big band show 'Top Score' featuring Alfred Marks, singers Diana Coupland, Marie Benson and Dick James, Steve Race and trumpeter Eddie Calvert. The producer was Johnnie Stewart and all the music was arranged by Stanley Black.

In some ways I found 'Much Binding in the Marsh' a funny show, apart from the script. The late Sam Costa, for example, was popular with the listeners but he never hàd much of a part. He would sometimes complain to me – as if I could do anything about it – that following his opening line, 'Good mornin' – was there somethink', he didn't have as many words to speak during the rest of the show. I suppose he got some relief from being able to talk to someone about his lack of lines. Then there was Kenneth Horne, with his chauffeur driven Rolls Royce parked outside the studios, who would frequently approach me for a tenor reed – 'one that you don't need' – when he could have bought one for himself for half-a-crown. When the Musicians' Social and Benevolent Council collection box was passed round each week, the usual donation was half-a-crown but he could never find more than sixpence! I remember that Richard 'Stinker' Murdoch played the fife on the show while Kenneth Horne made the most unmusical sound on the tenor sax – a nice man for all that – much to the delight of the studio audience.

Somewhat to our surprise, on 28 December 1948 we played this show before Princess Elizabeth and Princess Margaret, who sat in the front row of the audience, their voices ringing with laughter at what turned out to be one of their favourite radio programmes.

During another recording of the show I spotted an old acquaintance from my

RAF years sitting in the audience – S/Ldr 'Admin' Morice. When the recording finished I went down to have a chat with him and his friends, all friends of Kenneth Horne who had himself held a wartime commission in the RAF. Kenneth joined us, saying to Morice, 'I'd like you to meet one of *my* boys' little realising that we had known each other at Wittering for more than two years.

One of the most popular radio series was 'Ray's A Laugh', which had a witty and clever script, most of which was written by Ted Ray himself. The supporting team included those two brilliant character actresses Patricia Hayes and Kitty Bluitt. Kitty was very well liked by the boys in the band – Harry Hunter had a fancy for her – and indeed it was a happy show with Ted's wife attending the rehearsals, wearing those extraordinary hats which so amused us. Sons Robin and Andrew usually accompanied their mother, and Tessa too would often come along, usually at the conclusion of a West End 'shopping spree'.

The one radio series I would gladly have played for without any payment was 'Life With The Lyons'. The Lyon family – Bebe Daniels, Ben Lyon, daughter Barbara and adopted son Richard – were such warm and friendly people to work with in a show that was for the most part scripted by Bebe Daniels. Of all the radio performers I have played for, this family was perhaps the ultimate in professionalism with their acute sense of timing and excellent delivery. They took meticulous care over the scripts, which they taped during rehearsals so that at each break they could listen over in Ben's dressing room, making notes of any adjustments that might be required. The tape of course included the musical backing and should not have been made as the taping of music was breaking a rule of the Musicians' Union. However, this family was so admired and respected that we looked the other way and never made an issue of it.

For one of these broadcasts before a specially invited audience of show business celebrities, senior producers and directors of the BBC, the Paris Cinema Studios were redecorated, with new signs posted on the doors of the cloakrooms and toilets, together with a new set of direction signs placed along the walls. As I sat alone in the lower lounge before the broadcast a sudden thought came into my head and, without further thought, I began to switch all the signs round! I then resumed my seat and waited. The first celebrity to come down the main stairs was the actress Valerie Hobson. When she entered the 'GENTS' to use the telephone I quickly moved away from the immediate area. I did not want any awkward questions! From a safer distance I watched the increasing chaos that developed over the next ten minutes or so as more celebrities came down and whizzed in and out of doors as in a bedroom farce! Eventually the head porter arrived to sort out the confusion. It was a harmless 'lumber' which the Lyon family in particular seemed to find amusing. Harry Hunter gave me a questioning look, but I refused to confirm his suspicions.

A radio series consisted of 13 programmes and after the last one, without fail, a party would be arranged for the artists, the technicians and the orchestra members. These parties were held either on stage in the studio or in the nearest pub – usually in a private room of The Captain's Cabin in the Haymarket. At the end of the 'Life With The Lyons' series, Ben and Bebe gave their party at which she reminisced about her early days in Hollywood, working with Harold Lloyd, Dick Powell, Ruby Keeler, Alice Faye and the comedy team of Wheeler and Wolsey. She knew all the Hollywood greats including Gloria Swanson, Mary Pickford and Douglas Fairbanks Snr.

There is one radio series programme that I particularly recall. This was in October 1948 when we recorded one of the shows in Portsmouth before an audience of 800 sailors. That night we backed, among others, singer Gerry Brererton, who thought that his opportunity had passed him by when he was blinded during the war. The name of the show – 'Opportunity Knocks'!

Several American artistes were very appreciative of Stanley Black's backings for their radio shows, among them Dorothy Dandridge, the well-known singer-actress, who was also accompanied by her own bassist, drummer and pianist. Her sentiments were echoed by the Merry Macs, the top close harmony group who were originally founded by the McMichael brothers and now included 'local boy' Clive Erard, one-time member of Ambrose's Rhythm Boys who had taken part in that memorable concert at the Royal Opera House some 20 years before. The composer David Rose was greatly impressed with the quality of the string section when we recorded his *Holiday for Strings*, after which Stanley Black introduced him to us, with surprise and pleasure on both sides. During the break our leader, John Davis, Bert Bullimore, Bill Glover and I, in the course of a conversation learned that although he was known as a famous Hollywood composer-conductor-arranger, David Rose was in fact a Cockney born within the sound of Bow Bells.

I told David Rose a little story about the time when the Glenn Miller USAAF band was over here in 1944. The occasion was one of those British–American parties in London when I was with Geraldo's orchestra. At the party Maurice Burman was threading his way down a staircase crowded with musicians and girls drinking and chatting when he was intrigued to overhear a conversation between Dave Rose (one of Sam Donahue's arrangers for the US Navy Band) and a pretty, sweet-voiced young blonde. She was saying, '. . . how clever of you to have written *Holiday for Strings*, it's such a catchy piece of music. . . ', with Dave replying, 'Well, it's just one of those things, doll . . .', when Dave, who was obviously trying to make it with her under false pretences, however unintended, happened to look up and catch Maurice's eye and quickly changed the conversation! David Rose, much amused by the tale, said to me with a smile – 'Well, it's just one of those things!'

At another recording session at the Aeolian Hall a few of us from the orchestra met up with Harry Gold and his Pieces of Eight during a tea break. As I sat with them drinking my tea I turned casually away to say 'Hello' to someone nearby and as I did so, unknown to me, Harry's brother Laurie (the tenor player) dropped something into my tea. I chatted merrily on until I drained the cup, whereupon I was stunned to see a glass eye staring up at me from the bottom of it! Amid roars of laughter Laurie made a grab for the eye; but recovering my senses I beat him to it and snatching up the cup ran out of the canteen. In all the years I had known

Laurie Gold I had never realised that he wore a glass eye. Laurie gave chase with one hand over his empty eye-socket, but I escaped him until a while later I relented and returned it: I couldn't have let him go through a session without his false eye.

On 29 October 1951 the Stanley Black BBC Orchestra augmented to 29 pieces and under the leadership of John Davis, appeared in the Royal Command Performance before King George VI and Queen Elizabeth at the Victoria Palace in aid of the Variety Artists' Benevolent Fund. Harry Hunter, Manny Winters, Jimmy Durant and Les Perry were with me in the reed section that evening. The dance band world was also represented by a Keyboard Quintet comprising Carroll Gibbons, Billy Thorburn, Charlie Kunz, Ivor Moreton and Dave Kaye, the vocal touch being supplied by Vera Lynn and Sam Browne and his Singers. I still treasure my card of congratulations on being selected, which was sent by the presenter of the show, Jack Hylton, Prince Littler and Harry Marlowe, president and secretary respectively of the Fund and Institution.

One day in 1952 the band call was in a small downstairs room of the Piccadilly Studios, opposite the Piccadilly Hotel, where we were assembled for the recording of a trial run for a new radio show. The band set up with the saxes in front, everyone tooting away, myself most prominent of all. I was not being intentionally conspicuous: there was always something to be musically perfected and this was my way of achieving it – rather than sit on my backside wasting valuable time.

'Come over here, Peter,' I heard an unfamiliar voice call out; 'That's him,' the voice continued, its owner pointing at me. I wondered for a moment or two what I had done wrong or out of place. 'That's Billy Amstell,' the same chap emphasised with a glint in his eye that further unsettled me. 'Is it?' queried his companion. 'What have I done?' I protested, raising my voice. Still pointing at me the first character replied, 'I've read your articles in the *Melody Maker*.' 'Oh; is that all,' I mumbled, relieved. 'Spike's my name and this is Peter,' he informed me as we shook hands on this my first meeting with Spike Milligan and Peter Sellers, for this was the audition for 'The Goon Show'. Right from the outset the boys in the band and the studio technicians found the script fresh with a new style of radio humour which greatly appealed to everyone present.

Stanley Black, who chose the appropriate music, was I think the ideal person to be associated from the beginning with the series, considering his wide musical background and the fact that he too was a one-time 'lumberer'! The trial run proved to be a success and 'The Goon Show' was given three more programmes, broadcast from the Aeolian Hall, with a specially invited audience of family, friends, agents and a few 'wierdies'. Before the transmissions began the cast put on their own 'jam session' with Peter Sellers on drums, Spike Milligan on trumpet, Ray Ellington on bongoes, Max Geldray on harmonica and script writer Ray Galton on piano. The sessions opened, appropriately enough, with *When You're Smiling* and it all certainly warmed up the studio audience.

One evening I called on Peter Sellers, and as he opened the door of his flat I noticed that it was darker inside than outside. 'Come in', he invited me then changing his mind said, 'Let's go next door to Spike.' The bearded Milligan, with a piece of string hanging round his neck from which dangled a latchkey, asked: 'Well, what are you waiting for?' So Peter and I went in – to an even darker flat than Peter's! Once inside I found I was in the environment I so much enjoyed . . . sitting in the dark, listening to records, and having a drink or two. A Bob Crosby record was playing as we entered, to be followed by some by Artie Shaw, Benny Goodman and the Dorsey Brothers. We sat there . . . taking a sip of our drinks . . . seldom speaking . . . three lovers of jazz.

I think Spike Milligan has a natural feeling for jazz, and if he had devoted more time to practice he would have made an excellent jazz trumpeter. More or less the same could be said of Peter Sellers, who gained a lot of experience playing drums in the RAF, as well as on short-term engagements with the bands of Oscar Rabin and Henry Hall. As we know now, further 'Goon Shows' followed and there was no holding them back – Peter and Spike, Harry Secombe and Michael Bentine. Spike kindly mentioned me in his book, *Adolph Hitler; My Part in his Downfall*, although he did describe me as a Sergeant of Artillery instead of as a bandsergeant in the RAF with very little service training . . . though it made no difference . . . we still won the war!

Most of the radio series were repeated over the air at various times – some of them many years later at the time of the BBC's 50th and 60th anniversaries in 1972 and 1982. The extra income derived from repeats was most welcome – it still is! – for the BBC was never in the top league when it came to paying musicians. There were, however, other little extras, such as the payment of one guinea (£1.05p) when on the odd occasion I played a solo which meant leaving my seat in the orchestra in order to get up close to the microphone.

Those series which were sold abroad also attracted an extra payment, so all in all, it was a quite enjoyable way of making a living – having fun and getting paid for it!

Early in October 1952 the BBC gave the Stanley Black Orchestra three months notice and we finished on 2 January 1953, giving way to the Cyril Stapleton Show Band. Harry Hunter remarked to me at the time – 'you know how it is, Billy; as one door closes, another door shuts!' In this case, however, the door was 'ajar', for Stanley Black was taking a band out on tour, by public demand.

23 'Nice Work If You Can Get It'

Apart from playing in Stanley Black's BBC Orchestra I was also engaged to play for other programmes, although permission always had to be obtained from the orchestra manageress, Ann Asplin. Johnnie Stewart produced the Saturday night Jazz Club series and obtained authority for me to play on many of these dates. One such programme was in the nature of a reunion: Johnnie asked me to assemble my original RAF Quintet with Arthur Mouncey, Bobby McGee, Sid Heiger and Tiny Winters. This 30-minute broadcast also included the Far East Quintet featuring George Chisholm (tb); Alan Wood (as, cl); Ike Isaacs (g) and Charles Judah (vcl). Another series I took part in was the Jazz Club from Bush House to France, produced by Robin Scutt who later became head of BBC TV. Then one of the progressive producers, Charles Chiltern, put on a series of hour long musical shows entitled 'Golden Age', the theme of which was mainly Mississippi type jazz of the early 1930s with arrangements by Alf Ralston. Charles Chiltern secured permission for me to play clarinet in the BBC Revue Orchestra.

On one of the Jazz Club programmes we were at a loss to find a suitable jazz tune to feature both Freddy Gardner and myself until Freddy suggested *Farewell Blues*. So we took a chorus each, then 16 bars each, but I was too *pianissimo* and I was told to get up to the microphone with Freddy. As I was at least a foot shorter than him I was in something of a predicament, which caused a certain amount of amusement among the rest of the band. Freddy was such a likeable fellow, much admired throughout the profession, that we were all shocked and saddened to learn of his sudden passing only a few days later. I was so affected that I dreamt of him and one day when I was in the company of Captain Fred Stone, brother of Lew Stone and a confirmed believer in spiritualism, Fred expressed his belief that the spirit of Freddy Gardner was at my side . . . I was not in the least surprised.

Looking back to the late 1940s and early 1950s I see these as the busiest of my career. During my first three months with Stanley Black I did a whole lot of outside work which comes from my diary something like this –

11 & 18 October: Gig at a private function with my Quartet consisting of Jack Drummond (p); Teddy Wadmore (b); Micky Greeves (d) and myself on clarinet.

14 October: Played tenor sax with the London Symphony Orchestra at the Royal Albert Hall.

17 October: Played tenor sax and clarinet for London Symphony Orchestra at Denham Film Studios.

22 October: Joined forces once again with Nat Allen, who featured me on a TV show playing my composition *Don't Fuss* on clarinet.

During November and December I played dates with Ambrose and Van Straten plus a number with my own band, finishing on New Year's Eve at the Café Royal where my band played from 8pm until 2am after I had spent all day in the BBC studios with Stanley Black's Orchestra!

It was much the same through the whole of 1948, when I played for several bandleaders – at the Milroy Club with Paul Adam; at Grosvenor House with Tommy Kinsman;* at Ciro's Club for Maurice Winnick; at Churchill's Club for Jack Nathan (it was here that someone in the band 'lumbered' me by kindly letting the air out of one of my tyres). I also played a few dates for Victor Sylvester at the Hammersmith, which musically I found most unrewarding. He was a charming man, but how could he conduct on the up-beat when it should have been on the down-beat? Further work came my way when I played a number of times in the orchestra at the London Collesium for *Annie Get Your Gun* where the MD was Lew Stone. Then I played three sessions at Denham with the LSO as well as broadcasting with them from the Maida Vale studios, where the conductor was Stanford Robinson, a most impressive young man with an abundant knowledge of music. And all through the year I was playing gigs with my own band.

At the end of August 1948 Tessa and I spent a two week holiday near Lugano. Flying to Zürich we broke our journey there to pay a visit to Maurice Burman who was receiving treatment in a clinic. At Zürich Airport on the way home we met Eddie Bruenner, one time tenor player with Louis de Vries who had sat beside my brother Mick, Freddy Schweitzer and Melle Weersma. I recall that Freddy, a German-born saxophonist and clarinettist who was also the 'Funny man' in Jack Hylton's band, was playing for Jack in the early days of the war when he was taken in by the police for questioning. Melle Weersma had been one of Jack Hylton's pre-war staff arrangers.

Early that autumn I was the subject of the 'Personal Points' feature in *Melody Maker* in which my particular musical tastes were listed as musicians: Benny Goodman and Mel Powell; bands: Stan Kenton and Woody Herman; recordings: Kenton's *Concerto to End All Concertos* and Victor Young's *Tubby the Tuba*; composers: George Gershwin and Mendelssohn; arrangers: Eddie Sauter and Ken Thorne. If I were to be asked the same questions 35 years on, my answers would

---

*That year I played alongside tenor saxophonist Don Barrigo on a few recording sessions for Tommy Kinsman. Don, who we nicknamed 'Baron' because of his imposing appearance, had been one of Nat Gonella's original Georgians back in 1934, and during the middle and late 1930s also played for Lew Stone and Maurice Winnick. He was a handsome chap in a rugged sort of way, full of charm and a keep-fit fanatic, besides which he possessed a sharp sense of humour, enjoyed a prank or two, and had a roving eye for the girls. One of his little jokes was to hire a chauffeur driven car, drive to the Astoria in Charing Cross Road, and once inside start chatting up the girls. At a pre-arranged time the chauffeur would enter the ballroom, respectfully approach Don, and say, 'Your car awaits you, Baron'. It may have been a trifle expensive but it was a surefire way of 'making the birds!' At the end of 1948 Don Barrigo emigrated to South Africa where he opened a health and pleasure resort near Johannesburg.

not be very different though I would add Artie Shaw, 'Peanuts' Hucko and Oscar Peterson.

That November, Ambrose's secretary Joan Linton telephoned me to say that Bert wanted to see me at his office as soon as possible. When I arrived he told me: 'We're starting up again, Billy.' My thoughts flew back to the days at Ciro's Club, playing from 9pm until 2am and remembering how I had left Geraldo to play there and then really wished I hadn't. My career was going well, plenty of sessions, my own ORBS programmes, playing for the radio series; working hard and, as I said before, having fun and being paid for it. I think I mumbled, 'Lovely, Bert –' whereupon Ambrose observed, 'I can see you're not too keen, Billy.' 'It's not that, Bert,' I told him; 'It's those darned late nights all over again.' Soothing my embarrassment he said quickly, 'You're a good boy, Billy' – his favourite expression if he liked you – 'You stay with Stanley Black.' 'You don't mind, Bert?' I apologised rather than asked. 'No, no, Billy. Have another cup of coffee.' My old friend finished our conversation.

The following week Teddy Hayes, violinist in one of the BBC orchestras, asked me if I would give his young son Brian some lessons on the alto sax. Although I was busy and not at that time enthusiastic about teaching I agreed to give the lad some tuition at my home. He began his lessons during the Christmas school holidays. His mother brought him each time, and after only a few lessons I realised that this plump young lad had a real aptitude for playing the saxophone. He continued to practice and progressed rapidly. As he grew up he was no longer called Brian but 'Tubby' – yes, the late Tubby Hayes who became the finest tenor saxophone player in this country apart, perhaps, from Ronnie Scott. At the height of his career I came across Tubby one day at the BBC and jokingly asked him if he would give me some lessons!

Early in the following March Benny Goodman's brother Harry came over here for a short holiday. When we met I gave him three of my compositions and was cheered to hear that when he returned to the States he lost no time in passing them on to his famous brother. As well as my numbers being 'plugged' in the US, French bandleader Bernard Hilda had as many as 17, all of them being played by his band at Ciro's Club. It certainly seems that he had acquired a taste for my kind of music and I was invited to meet him. We met at Pastori's, a small exclusive hotel in Leicester Square owned by the same Mr Pastori who was manager at the Grosvenor House Hotel when I was playing there in 1930/31. Hilda and I had a few drinks, and then he went off to play at Ciro's. As a bandleader he had his own (possibly unique) method of encouraging couples to take to the dance floor: if no one was dancing he would approach the nearest lady to him and request a dance. As soon as he had taken the floor, literally with the first step others followed.

Later in the month I was heartened to read in *Melody Maker* that I was fast earning the title of 'Britain's Ambassador of Song'! At the time I had just written another number with Ralph Sharon, entitled *It Might as Well Be-bop* while Stanley Black had recently featured my arrangement of my own *Jumpin'* over the air.

Shortly afterwards Billy Ternent and his Band broadcast the same piece form the Kilburn Empire.

During the summer I was deeply saddened to hear of the death of my old friend and colleague from the pre-war Ambrose days, Danny Polo, who died suddenly in the studio while playing in the Claude Thornhill orchestra. He had suffered a cerebral haemorrhage on 11 July, shortly after returning to the Thornhill orchestra. After leaving Ambrose in 1938 he was playing in the Ray Ventura band on the Continent when war broke out. He sailed from Bordeaux on the last ship to leave France for the USA and when he arrived in New York joined Joe Sullivan's band before going over to Jack Teagarden prior to his first spell with Thornhill. It was, however, his wonderful work with Ambrose that assured him the affectionate remembrance of all the musicians and fans who were privileged to hear him. I consider myself fortunate to have played alongside Danny for longer than any other musician in any band, anywhere. Over the years I received postcards from him asking about his former friends and colleagues in this country. I continue to prize and use the clarinet he gave me. He was only 47 when he died.

I first saw and heard Benny Goodman give a 'live' performance when Maurice Burman, Jack Nathan and I went to the London Palladium on 23 July. We had seats in the front row, and I well remember how Benny positioned himself not far from his pianist, Buddy Greco, with his clarinet right up to the microphone and the complete ease with which he played. I had been invited by Tony Brown, Technical Editor of *Melody Maker* to become the first musician to interview Benny Goodman and it was scheduled to take place during his Palladium engagement. Before that, however, I met Benny at the Paris Cinema Studios where he was appearing on one of the episodes of 'High Gang', which starred Bebe Daniels, Ben Lyon and Vic Oliver. Guesting on the show Benny quipped, 'I always promised myself that one day I'd give up the clarinet and sing – would you like to try me out?' Ben Lyon gave him the go-ahead and Benny sang *Put Your Shoes On Lucy*. This was the first time we in Britain had ever heard Benny Goodman sing. When he had finished, Ben Lyon cracked: 'Now we've heard you sing, a word of advice if I may – don't sell your clarinet, Benny!' Goodman then played several choruses of *The World is Waiting for the Sunrise*, one of which I chose to copy out for printing in *Melody Maker*.

I didn't want to bore him with small talk, so I simply told him that *Melody Maker* had asked me to prepare a questionnaire for a planned interview to take place the following week at the Palladium. 'Why can't we do it now?' he asked me. I replied that I had not finished preparing the questions, whereupon he said, 'OK, man, see you next week.' 'Very well, Mr Goodman,' I rather formally responded. For some reason I could not bring myself to address him as 'Benny'. It is difficult to explain why I couldn't: remember that it was some time before I could bring myself to call Bert Ambrose anything but 'Mr Ambrose'; perhaps that had something to do with it, though I never experienced any such difficulty when I met Jimmy Dorsey, Artie Shaw or Michael Hucko. Nor am I quite sure why I was selected to interview Benny Goodman. It may have been because I had played the role of 'BG' on the BBC Jazz Club radio programme, just prior to the great man's visit; or perhaps it was because it was well known that I had collected all his records from the earliest days – or was it because I had written several numbers in the Goodman style and dedicated one to him?

At the interview Benny looked astonished when I produced a manuscript of the original chorus of *China Boy*, which Stanley Black had taken down at the time when the recording, made with Red Nichols, was first issued. He studied the manuscript, humming softly; then: 'Yeah! That's it,' he smiled, 'they seem to like that chorus over here.' I then took down a clarinet chorus of *The World is Waiting for the Sunrise* which he played over the radio at the extremely fast tempo and dedicated to the readers of *Melody Maker*.

Benny was delighted when I next produced a small band arrangement of my own composition *Benny's Shadow*. When he asked if he might keep it, I replied: 'Of course. I thought you'd never ask!' Meeting Benny Goodman was the highlight of the year, if not of my entire career.

Early in October I was asked to 'turn the key' and officially open the Chas Club at the Swan Hotel in Stockwell. Those present included Johnnie Stewart and London Jazz Club personality Bert Wilcox, who in a few years was to produce two of my LPs. Also present that night was the Hon Gerald Lascelles, brother of the Earl of Harewood and a great jazz lover whose favourite instrument was the clarinet. A pleasant, friendly fellow, he always addressed me as 'half-pint' and I recall that he invariably offered his cigarettes around in a small tin box, the kind normally used for throat lozenges!

By the end of the 1940s you might say I was in the export business, for my compositions were being played not only by progressively minded bandleaders in Britain but also by Bernard Hilda in Paris and recorded in Australia by Paul Lombard. In October 1948 I had formed Modern Music (London) Ltd – probably the only non-commercial music publishing house in the world, catering entirely for musicians. The late Jimmy Phillips, managing director of the Peter Maurice Music Company, gave me the encouragement to go into the music publishing business. I had written and arranged at least a dozen small band jazz numbers, including *Benny's Shadow*, *Up and Down the Scale*, *Stick of Liquorice*, *Tootin' Around* and *Don't Fuss*, and Jimmy, being a good friend, planted the seed, although it was my idea to publish 'A British Catalogue'. He was kind enough to return my composition *The Joint's A-Jivin'* so that I could publish it despite the fact that having sent the number to Dave Rose (of the US Navy Band) in the States to be slightly rearranged, it had cost him $100. Our list of composers included Ralph Sharon, Malcolm Mitchell, Roy Plumber, Kenny Baker, Sid Phillips, Harry Gold, Johnny Dankworth, Norrie Paramor, Dizzy Reece and Tony Crombie.

A year later Jimmy introduced me to New York music publisher Jack Mills, brother of Irving Mills, part time composer and a former agent for Duke Ellington, Cab Calloway and other top line American bands. I took Kenny Baker, Malcolm Mitchell and Ralph Sharon along with me to meet Jack, who bought two of our works (which we had already published here). Soon after he arrived back in

New York he cabled to say that he would publish eight of our British speciality numbers in the States, including Ralph Sharon's *Bella*, Johnny Dankworth's *Domerus* and my own *Sweetest Thing*. It was around this time too that Joe Crossman and I opened a musical instrument shop in the West End, although after a year or so Joe tired of it – I think it interfered with his tennis!

Apart from playing and publishing I was being kept busy writing at the end of the 1940s and into the 1950s. In the summer of 1949 *Melody Maker* asked me to take over answering technical enquiries received from sax and clarinet players from the late Freddy Gardner. I not only wrote this weekly spot but also contributed some stories and memoirs. Then in October of that year, at the behest of Jack Baverstock, editor of the monthly magazine *Music Fare*, I took over the reviewing of radio broadcasts of dance and jazz bands from saxophonist/arranger George Evans. My first assignment included reviewing a broadcast by one of my old leaders – Bert Ambrose! While radio critics are supposed to criticise the performances on the air, I took the unusual step of reviewing Sid Dean's big band – I say 'big' because I recall that there were five saxes and six brass in the lineup – 'in the flesh'. It so happened that Tessa and I were on holiday at Rottingdean and I thought it would be a good idea to go along to the Regent Ballroom in Brighton and do my job on the spot. While there producer Frank Hooper invited me into the control room where I continued to take notes of Sid's band on the air. A young girl singer, a newcomer to the band, sang that night in front of more than 1600 fans, hundreds of them crowded round the bandstand – her name was Jill Day. The young man delivering the programme announcements was David Jacobs.

Expressing my honest opinions in a forthright way, however, by no means endeared me to some of the bandleaders or their bands. I wrote of a Harry Roy broadcast on one occasion, '. . . I wonder if his style will ever come back? . . .' I referred of course to his clarinet playing. Soon after my review appeared I came across him in Park Lane, chatting with Maurice Winnick, and when I said 'Hello' he completely ignored me.

It was in April 1950 that the American impressario and record producer Norman Granz, sponsor of Jazz At The Philharmonic, flew into London for 24 hours, and I was among a handful of musicians and musical personalities who met him at Bosworth's, the music publishers. Ted Heath, tenor sax player Don Rendell, Johnny Dankworth, Ralph Sharon and Edgar Jackson were there with me to enjoy recordings of the great Charlie Parker and an exciting young Canadian pianist by the name of Oscar Peterson. Norman Granz told us that Charlie Parker's recording of *April in Paris*, with strings, took three days to make due to Charlie's shyness at playing in the company of 'long hairs'. Eventually they got on friendly terms and Charlie was able to relax and, in Granz's words, 'give with the music'. It was my good fortune to be given a copy of this record which I still have. Indeed, I have every record I ever bought since those days in Louis Freeman's shop in Glasgow at the end of the 1920s. Norman Granz's only other date during that brief London visit was with 'his tailor', who he said has been recommended to him by Fred Astaire. On that recommendation he ordered seven suits!

Right:
27 With Geraldo's Orchestra in Brussels (November 1944) Drummer, Maurice Burman

Below:
28 On the way to Monte Carlo (1946) Malcolm Lockyer, Alan Metcalfe, Aubrey Frank, Max Goldberg, Lew Carew

Above:
29 Tessa at the New Beach
Hotel, Monte Carlo (July 1946)
J. Stara, Paris

Right:
30 Billy and Tessa with Sid
Simone and wife Dinah, New
Beach Hotel, Monte Carlo (July
1946)

31 Peanuts Hucko

32 With Johnny Dankworth, Barry Ulanov and Harold Davison

33 At Bush House: 'Overseas to France' . . . Jazz date (*c1947*)
Robin Scott (producer); Arthur Mouncey (t); George Chisholm (tb); Mike McKenzie (p); Tiny
Winters (b); Billy with clarinet; Jock Cummings (d); Joe Denise (g)

34 Band for one of the ORBS broadcasts 'The Amstell Way' (1947)
Left to right: Alan Metcalfe, Norman Burns, Malcolm Lockyer, Ronnie Peters, Alan Dean, David Jacobs, Billy

Above left:

35 At IBC Studios (May 1947)

Left to right: Ron Peters, Billy, David Jacobs (with 'posh' accent), Norman Burns, Alan Dean, Malcom Lockyer, Alan Metcalfe

Below left:

36 With Benny Goodman and Tony Brown (Technical editor of *Melody Maker*) (July 1949)

Above:

37 Stockwell Jazz Club (October 1949)

Extreme left, BBC Producer Johnnie Stewart; right, Billy with Bert Wilcox, Chairman and Secretary of Club

Below:

38 With Malcolm Mitchell, Ralph Sharon, Jack Mills and Kenny Baker, at the Dorchester Hotel (1949)

39 With the Stanley Black Orchestra at the Royal Command Performance (1951)

40 Tessa and Billy with Kenny Graham and Leslie 'Jiver' Hutchinson

41 Dickie Valentine and family (1958)

Above:

42 The Queen dancing to the music of Tommy Kinsman's Band at the Hyde Park Hotel, London, on the occasion of the centenary of the Battle of Balaclava (1954)

Above right:

43 George Chisholm's Jazzers (for The Black and White Minstrels Show), (January 1960)
Left to right: George Chisholm, Billy, Jackie Peach, Gordon Franks, Lenny Bush, Tommy McQuater.

Sidney W. Baynton

Below right:

44 Chisholm's Jazzers (March 1960)
Left to right: Jackie Peach, George Chisholm, Lenny Bush, Billy, Jack Emblow, Tommy McQuater.

Sidney W. Baynton

s.s. CANBERRA

P&O

Commodore F. B. Woolley, R. D., R.N.R.
Deputy Captain D. J. Scott Masson, R.D., R.N.R.
and Officers

request the pleasure of your company

in the

Meridian Room on the Promenade Deck

Sunday 26 November 1978

Passengers on First Sitting from 6.30 p.m. until 7.00 p.m.
Passengers on Second Sitting from 7.45 p.m. until 8.15 p.m.

s.s. Canberra

Far left:
45 Souvenir of the cruise on
SS Canberra (1978)

Left:
46 Ernest M. Morial, Mayor
of New Orleans

Below:
47 The works of Billy
M. Aramaz

Above:
48 *Memory Lane* Party,
Manchester (June 1984)
Left to right: Alan Dell, Billy
Munn, Tiny Winters, Joe
Daniels (seated), Tommy
McQuater, Billy, Andy
Carnochan (host)
Manchester Evening News

Left:
49 Billy and Tessa at home
(1985)
Informer Group

Above:
50 Billy and Tessa with Flt/Lt
Keith Williams CRO after
lunch in the Officers' Mess at
RAF Wittering (30 August
1985)

Right:
51 Billy Amstell at the Foyer
of the Royal Festival Hall
(1985)
M. Aramaz

52 Tessa and Billy with Flt/Lt Andy Delabar revisiting the 'scene of crime'
Stamford Photographic Services

Mention of Charlie Parker reminds me of a visit in the later summer of 1950 of Barry Ulanov, with George T. Simon co-editor of the American musical monthly *Metronome*. Barry was over here to review the jazz scene in Britain, and his subsequent article, printed in the October issue of *Metronome*, was entitled, 'Right-ho! That's Jazz in Great Britain: crawling with scrubbers,** frightfully posh and full of talented geezers'. In his story Barry wrote of his thoughtful discussions 'with Maurice Burman . . . and with Billy Amstell, a very active clarinettist who removes highly reputable playing from the conversation in order to analyse more penetratingly the drama of be-bop, which he likes but can't play (he says), or the comedy of Dixieland, which he knows he plays well, but doesn't like quite so much.'

**American expression for a band's female hangers-on.

24 On Tour With Stanley Black

Early in 1953 I was one of only three or four musicians to make the transition from Stanley Black's BBC Orchestra to his touring band. This latter was reduced in personnel and took the form of a big band without strings. We were replaced at the BBC by the Cyril Stapleton Show Band, although some of his touring musicians, including pianist/arranger Ken Jones, elected to join Stanley Black. Bill Povey led the sax section which included that lovely, stylish tenor player Johnny Evans as well as Derek Grossmith and myself and later Paul Bennett. Frank Thornton led the brass on trumpet, and former Jack Payne stalwart Bert Bullimore was also in the section.

The featured vocalists were Diana Coupland, Monty Norman and Martin Moreno, with Alma Warren replacing Diana later in the tour. Diana and Monty were inseparable and it came as no surprise to any of us when they eventually got married. Both went on to develop their respective talents in other fields, Diana as an actress in serious and light comedy roles, mostly on TV, while Monty devoted his time to writing for the theatre. Alma Warren, sister of Lita Roza, singer with the Ted Heath band, was a beautiful looking girl with a most appealing voice, and was always a pleasure to work with. Some years ago she became secretary to the American music publishers, Leeds Music Ltd. Martin Moreno, a handsome Latin–American looking type who played percussion and sang in Spanish, was actually born George Richards and like me was a Cockney!

Stanley Black always opened the second half of our concerts with a splendid arrangement of *When the Saints Go Marching In* in which I was well featured on clarinet. He also used this number to audition my replacement some 15 months later after I had handed in my notice. To finish our concerts the band played Stanley's unique arrangement of the National Anthem, which began softly with five woodwind and, as the brass joined in, gradually grew louder.

We worked mostly four days each week out of London although each time we returned to town there were radio and TV dates to fulfil. The Scottish tour in particular was very demanding: it took in Kilmarnock, Dundee, Aberdeen, Inverness (which brought back memories of my RAF days at Invergordon), Falkirk and Kirkaldy. The pace was indeed hectic for we played six consecutive one-night stands north of the border. When travelling through the night after a 'one-nighter' during the winter, we were issued with a blanket apiece on the coach, and if anyone took somebody else's blanket, our bassist Frank Clark would give them the 'death-eye' and clamp down on the miscreant. On the way back to London we played on successive nights in Morecombe and Fleetwood, followed by a BBC radio date on our first day back in the capital, and then took part in a charity concert at the Stoll Theatre in aid of the victims of the disastrous floods of March 1953. Thankfully, the next two days were 'rest days': two engagements were cancelled in late March due to the death of Queen Mary – the first that night at Grosvenor House, the second the following night in Leeds.

When the tour took the band to Newcastle I realised that we were in the home town of Willie Walker who was in the Stanley Black BBC Orchestra when I first joined. It was widely known in musicians' circles that Willie was leading his trio at Fennick's, one of the largest stores in the city, so I took Johnny Evans, Derek Grossmith, Oscar Birch and Paul Bennett to hear him.

We made our way to a table near the bandstand where Willie recognised me, and when the opportunity arose I introduced him to my fellow reed players. He asked if there was any tune we would particularly like him to play and I suggested something with verve or zest. 'How about *Tico, Tico*? he enquired – and we agreed. He played the piece at a very fast tempo, every note single-tongued, leaving us more than impressed. 'Anything else?' he wanted to know. More or less in fun I asked this classically trained musician if he would play the famous old standard *If I Had You*. He played it superbly, his tone the equal to the best of the American clarinettists, and with more than a touch of Benny Goodman's style and technique. My companions were suitably amazed!

I was able to celebrate my forty-second birthday at home as the band had only three dates out of town that week. Shortly afterwards we began recording a series of 30 programmes for Radio Luxembourg which starred the orchestra and Vera Lynn. A large string section was added for this and Stanley wrote some excellent arrangements backing Vera. He also commissioned our pianist Ken Jones to write some arrangements for these shows and one evening Ken spent at least an hour on the telephone dictating the notes of a special chorus he wanted me to play in my particular style on clarinet. When I played it back to him he was delighted and the number was included in the next date. Within a few years Ken was to branch out on his own as a composer and arranger of theme music for films and TV.

The previous year Tessa and I had passed a most enjoyable holiday at a hotel on the Costa Brava, in the then tiny fishing village of Tossa del Mar which had been used as a location for the James Mason/Ava Gardner picture *Pandora and the Flying Dutchman* in 1951. We recommended the hotel to Ken Jones, his wife Betty, Diana Coupland and Monty Norman who acted on our recommendation. On the morning of their departure, Ken kindly telephoned me at 4am to let me know that they were on their way. Not being entirely happy about having my night's sleep disturbed like that, I muttered 'Go break a leg' into the telephone and went back to bed. Waiting to get my own back, I obtained some BBC notepaper and wrote to Ken asking him to attend a rehearsal for a Saturday Jazz Club date. He fell for it and cut his holiday short by a day!

Fifteen months of solid touring proved to be considerably more than enough for me. The musician who has a wife and maybe other family commitments tires of the life more quickly than the single man; furthermore, the attractions of travelling hundreds of miles on coaches, praying that the heating will not fail, suffering the vagaries of the British climate and living out of a suitcase in hotels and 'digs', are less than inviting, especially when one has done it all before with Ambrose, Geraldo and others and is past the age of 40. I knew only too well that I was missing Tessa as much as she was missing me, so on a one-night stand in Shrewsbury on 26 March 1954 I plucked up courage and asked Stanley Black if I might have a word with him during the break. He agreed and when the interval arrived I invited him into the bar and over drinks said, 'I'm sorry, Stanley, but I would like to finish.' Always one to think things over before he spoke – unlike me! – he paused before replying, 'I don't blame you – I wish I could.' He accepted my notice but had to continue touring himself for several months more before settling down to work in London.

My last date with the band took place at the Garrick Theatre on 11 April when we recorded a radio programme. The star of the show was the great Maurice Chevalier who remained on stage for more than two hours singing his best known songs, such as *You Brought a New Kind of Love to Me* and *Louise*. He was accorded a wonderful ovation but we were disappointed that the edited version of the recording was whittled down to 45 minutes. I do remember however that Chevalier was full of praise for our work for him.

That night I felt not a little sadness at leaving: I had been with the orchestra for six and a half years and, while it was none of my business, I couldn't help wondering who was going to take over my clarinet solo in *When the Saints Go Marching In* and *South Rampart Street Parade*, for example. Paul Bennett and Derek Grossmith were most proficient performers but not 'jazzers'.

At the end of the night the only musician to remain behind and wish me goodbye was my friend and fellow tenor player Johnny Evans. As I took my clarinet and tenor sax to the bandroom and lifted the lid of my instrument case, I noticed a package lying there. I opened it to find a small box of cigars from Johnny. Thinking what a charming old fashioned gesture it was, I smiled to myself, 'Good on him'.

Not long after I left the band toured Ireland, which some of the boys told me on their return was as tough as the Scottish tour had been. I was not sorry to have missed it, even though it did apparently have its funny side, like when a chap pulled at Stanley's trouser leg and asked if they played requests: on being invited to say what he would like he replied, 'Oh anything at all.'

25 Freelancing Again

As soon as I had left Stanley Black I returned once more to freelancing. I found I had plenty of work, playing BBC television dates with orchestra leaders Eric Robinson, Geoff Love and George Clouston, doing recording sessions with Bobby Mickleburgh's six-piece jazz group, plus some radio dates for Geraldo and the occasional broadcast and TV show for Steve Race. I also had some radio dates with Sid Phillips. Sid invited me to join his band on a permanent basis, but I declined because he was touring most of the time and playing at least three nights a week out of town.

In November 1954 I led a group which included Bobby Mickleburgh on trombone and Aubrey Frank on tenor which featured British jazz on the BBC Light Programme and was also relayed in the BBC Overseas Service. This brought a good deal of complimentary mail and I think this was partly responsible for me getting more 'Jazz Club' dates.

Once Stanley Black had finished touring I resumed working for him on some television shows. One of these I vividly remember; it starred the American comic Sid Caesar who, following a number of film appearances in the 1940s became a big hit on American TV in the 1950s. Co-starring with him in the BBC show was Imogene Coca, the American revue singer/comedienne who in the 1960s had her own TV show in the States. Their sheer professionalism made them a splendid team. Sid rarely appeared at rehearsals – except the penultimate one – and for one run through of a programme I stood in for him, playing the tenor saxophone in a rock and roll number. When he turned up at the dress rehearsal Sid was made up and dressed as a raving 'rocker', with shoulder-length hair and an exaggeratedly long jacket. Although his sax playing was on the rusty side, I could sense that he had at one time been a player of quality. During a break before the final rehearsal I chanced to pass his dressing room, the door of which was slightly open to reveal Sid relaxing on a sofa. 'Hello boichik,' he called out. 'What kind of mouthpiece do you use?' As the magic word 'boichik'* conveyed to me that he was a kindred spirit, he continued, 'Come on in.' I went into the room and told him that I used a Brilhart five Star. 'Great!' he exclaimed. 'That's exactly what I use.'

He then told me the story of how his first appearance in show business as a comic came about in New York's Radio City, where he was playing the saxophone in the orchestra for a radio show. Immediately before the broadcast began, the compère/ comedian collapsed and Sid, having something of a reputation of a 'bandroom

*Yiddish for 'laddie'.

comic', was called upon to fill the gap. So successful was he that the sponsors invited him to continue as comic in the series. So he gave up his career as a professional musician for that of comedian.

What really aroused my curiosity about Sid Caesar were the clothes he wore when he did appear at rehearsals – the frayed trousers, the old down at heel shoes which I could see quite clearly as he talked through his lines in front of the reed section. Feeling that such a pleasant, friendly chap would not think it too personal, I asked him about it. 'Oh those,' he replied. 'They were some of the clothes I wore when making my début as a professional comic – I wear them still for good luck and shall continue to do so, while they last!'

When I refused a cigarette, adding that I smoked only cigars, Sid said to me: 'Next week you shall have a nice cigar for standing in for me so well, boichik.' My thoughts went back some 25 years . . . to Jimmy Dorsey who wanted virtually to adopt me, so it seemed, and take me back to the States with him . . . and who knows? I might have become a comic . . . with a paste diamond studded clarinet!

It was while playing in the orchestra of Woolf Phillips in a BBC television show starring Vera Lynn that I met another American star. Vera's husband Harry Lewis came up to me and asked: 'Billy – would you like to meet Artie Shaw?' Before I could answer he grabbed me by the hand, saying, 'Come with me,' and then introduced me to one of my idols – a man who possessed one of the finest clarinet techniques, a most fluent player with a pleasing melodic approach. 'So you're the guy who used to play tenor in Ambrose's band,' Artie commented. For a moment I suspected that Harry Lewis had put him up to that opening line, so I replied cautiously, 'Yes, that's right.' 'Boy oh boy,' Shaw continued, 'that was a great band . . . I used to listen to it each week back home on the radio, Billy.' 'How nice of you to say so,' I rejoined, realising by now that he was quite sincere. 'May I call you Artie?' I asked him. 'I wouldn't have it any other way,' he responded with a grin. Time did not permit any further conversation, but there were a couple of other occasions 'when we met during his visit to this country and I remember talking with him about his former first alto player, Mac Pearce, who was a member of the US Navy Band when it came to England.

One story in particular about Artie Shaw appeals to me. Once, so Mac told me, after he had put away a few drinks Artie tried to figure out how he and the band could buy the hotel they were working in and run it on a co-operative basis. The snag was that when Artie was cold sober he could not remember anything about his alcoholic plan.

One day early in 1955 Tessa accepted on my behalf a recording session date at the HMV studios backing Spike Milligan. I was asked to take my clarinet along and as there was no mention of doubling on saxophone I got the feeling that I was in for an interesting session. Entering the Abbey Road studios I found myself among more than a score of 'gypsies', and so concluded that I was in the right place but at the wrong time! Then I spotted George Chisholm and Freddie Clayton in the crowd and asked them what was happening; but they seemed to know no more than I did. As we were chatting Norman Newell, lyricist and at that time recording manager, came running down the long staircase, calling out, 'Set up, boys.' As the well disciplined 'long hairs' did just that, George, Freddie and I were positioned around the microphone next to the rhythm section. We began running through the music, mostly of an orchestral nature, until a raving Spike Milligan stepped out from behind a screen (that was concealing another microphone), shouting, 'No, no, no. That's not what I want.' The 'gypsies' sat there looking scared . . . the tune we were playing seemed to be based on *Jerusalem*, although by this time it hardly seemed to make any difference what it was!

'The strings are too loud,' Spike announced emphatically; so Norman indicated to our leader, Geoff Love, that they should play softer still. Spike then disappeared behind the screen again, and as we continued rehearsing, he yelled out, 'Aus-tral-ia, Aus-tral-ia!' in place of 'Jerusalem, Jerusalem.' Well, we hadn't got very far into the arrangement (if you could call it that) before Spike came running out and ordered the complete string section to stop playing, at the same time pleading with George, Freddie and me to 'jazz it up'.

The fiddle players sat there motionless, apparently horrified, as we 'went to town' as Spike wanted. When we had finished he bellowed, 'That's great, that's great,' while Norman Newell asked the string players, for whom it had been an easy but far from pleasant session, to pack up and leave. Then once more the three of us ran through the music, accompanied by Spike (from behind the screen again) crying, 'Aus-tral-ia, Aus-tral-ia!', followed by sounds of his trumpet. The whole affair was something of a fiasco; we never made a 'master', so naturally no recording was ever released of what was, after all, a really disastrous session. Had it all 'come together', it might well have taken off as the Goons had done a few years previously; but it was not to be.

Making our way out of the studios we could hear the sounds of Spike playing *Basin Street Blues* on his trumpet, gradually growing fainter and fainter; and I thought, not for the first time, that somewhere inside Spike Milligan there was a little Louis Armstrong trying to get out.

26 On The Town and At The Circus

During the latter half of the 1950s I played in Geoff Love's orchestra on many Radio Luxembourg programmes; these featured many popular artistes, including Matt Munro, Ann Shelton, Vera Lynn, Winifred Atwell, Pearl Carr and Teddy Johnson, Russ Conway, Dickie Valentine, The King Brothers, The Ink Spots (not four of them as originally but three) and Frankie Vaughan. The majority of the arrangements were scored by the band's pianist, Sid Hadden.

It was at the Wembley Town Hall on a show sponsored by Elder and Fyffes that I first took part in a radio programme as anything else than a musician. Jeffrey Everett, a senior director of Radio Luxembourg, summoned me from my place in the orchestra and asked if I was enjoying myself, at the same time peeling a banana and stuffing it into my mouth as I tried to answer. The audience and the boys in the band roared with laughter – even more so when he repeated the joke again and yet again, by which time I was heartily sick of bananas. Later, at the Luxembourg studio in Hertford Street, I retaliated by tying a dustbin lid to the rear bumper of his car, which did not endear him to the local residents when he drove off after a night session.

'The Bingo Show', on which singers Pearl Carr and Teddy Johnson were making a name for themselves, came to a premature end when a High Court ruling that the programme amounted to a form of gambling went against the sponsors. So the bread was taken out of our mouths! I particularly remember one session when Pearl and Teddy had come up from Brighton and Pearl announced that she had a headache. I volunteered to give her a bit of massage and manipulation of the neck and shoulders. I fancied myself as something of a 'healer', and no one was more astonished than I was when it worked!

The Luxembourg sessions were most enjoyable, with Geoff Love radiating a warmth which spread throughout the studio or wherever else we happened to be playing.

The first ever Saturday night ITV show was transmitted 'live' from the Embassy Club on 10 September 1955. Geoff Love's eight-piece band provided the music and the show, entitled *On The Town*, ran for 16 consecutive weeks at the Embassy before being transferred to other clubs and restaurants including the Café Royal, the Trocadero, the Criterion and the Coconut Grove, returning intermittently to the Embassy.

Our first Master of Ceremonies was the popular former trumpet playing bandleader, Jack Jackson, a thoroughly likeable personality who unfortunately had to resign when it was realised that he couldn't see the monitor without his spectacles. He was followed first by the Australian Ron Randell, of the pseudo-American accent, and then by Canadian Bernard Braden, already well known on radio.

Among the guests on one Saturday night show was the American bandleader Stan Kenton, to whom I made myself known by way of a card of introduction given to me by Barry Ulanov. As a welcome to Stan, we played his signature tune, *Artistry in Rhythm*. When I spoke to him during an interval he seemed genuinely pleased with our small band arrangement. This I could not understand. It was so far removed from his own version with its eight-piece punching brass and swinging drums. Perhaps he was just being polite!

Another welcome guest at the Embassy Club was André Astric, head of all entertainment in Monte Carlo, with whom I enjoyed chatting during the band interval, recalling our first meeting when I was in Monte with Ambrose. Geraldo, who was his guest that night, seemed surprised that André and I had often met over the years.

These ITV dates lasted for a whole year, by which time commercial television had become firmly established.

In November 1957 I was playing with Geoff Love at the Beaconsfield Film Studios where we were featured in the picture *6.5 Special* for which Geoff had written the score. It is not one of my happiest memories, for I played what I can only describe as the 'hooligan' tenor saxophone solos, with the microphone almost down the bell of my instrument . . . 'rock and roll' . . . the type of music I can do without!

More to my musical taste was a recording session with Geoff Love at the HMV studios where we backed an American singer who possessed a magnificent and powerful voice. As he was over here appearing on the West End stage the most convenient time to record was as late at night as possible, so it became in fact a midnight session. During a playback I found myself standing next to this tall, virile looking fair haired fellow, and as he looked down at me, at least a foot, all I could think of saying was, 'I used to be tall.' 'What happened?' he asked. 'I haven't been well lately,' I replied. As we continued talking, I learnt that he used to play the trombone in his college band before taking up a career as a singer/actor and changing his name from Harold to Howard . . . Keel.

I continued to freelance, working for many bandleaders, among them Jack Payne, Jack Hylton, Sid Phillips, Bob Sharples, Ben Frankel, Norrie Paramor, Cyril Orandel, Steve Race, Peter Knight and Eric Robinson. Apart from playing for television, films, radio and on records, I deputised in theatre orchestras for stage musicals such as *Blitz* and *Expresso Bongo*.

In between dates with Geoff Love I played in Eric Robinson's orchestra for BBC TV on the understanding that in the event of a double date, Geoff Love would have precedence. For one particular show the adagio team included Gershwin's *Rhapsody in Blue* in their act, but, much to their annoyance, found that the lead sax player was unable to play the clarinet cadenza. Eric came off his rostrum and, standing in front of the reed section, asked if anyone could play it? Having heard

Danny Polo play that cadenza so many times it had become a pet study of mine, and I had actually recorded it for Cyril Orandel. During the silence that followed, I was tempted to speak up. But just in time I realised how unprofessional it would have been for me to give Eric an answer to a question addressed to a group of professionals. So I kept silence, not wanting to fall out with my colleagues. If he had made an individual approach it would have been a different matter . . .

On one occasion at the end of a *Music for You* programme on BBC television, Eric's concluding announcement ended with, '. . . and we'll play some more stuff [!] for you next week.' A somewhat inglorious finish to a lovely artistic programme that had included Elisabeth Schwarzkopf and Yehudi Menuhin. When I stopped wincing I was reminded of the 'Geraldo School of Elocution'!

I was a member of the Peter Knight Orchestra, both for the long-running TV series, 'Spot the Tune' and for the Charlie Chaplin film *A King in New York*. Peter Knight's was the only score for the film that Chaplin judged to be suitable: seven others failed to meet with his approval. This judgment reinforced my belief that Peter Knight was one of the three best orchestrators in the business, the other two in my opinion being Stanley Black and Wally Stott.

During a break at the Shepperton Studios I chanced to have a word with Charlie Chaplin, on 1 May 1956. I asked him: 'How does it feel to be home again, Mr Chaplin?' Sticking his thumbs through the arm holes of his waistcoat, he stared at me, replying: 'Ah! There's an air of freedom here.' I was not so much surprised by his answer as amazed by the fact that after more than 45 years in the United States, he still retained a perfect English accent – and waistcoat.

Towards the end of the summer of 1959 George Chisholm was asked to form a six-piece band to do a spot in the BBC television series, 'The Black and White Minstrel Show'. The series commenced in September, with George on trombone, Tommy McQuater (t); Jack Emblow (accordion); Jack Peach (d); Lenny Bush (later Jack Fallon) (b) and myself on clarinet. We assumed various disguises on stage, dressed as American GIs, Irish navvies, Canadian Mounted Police or Chinese Mandarins etc. For some reason I was instantly recognisable whatever I wore and the producer, George Inns, thought I looked very comical, dubbed me 'Ginsberg of the Mounties' and 'the Chief Rabbi of Singapore'!* The series ran for over two years during which time our little outfit recorded for EMI and made an appearance in Chipperfields's Circus. This latter came about because the circus was to be televised and the producer thought it appropriate to insert a spot for a small jazz group into the show.

So on 28 August 1960 we arrived at Kingston-upon-Thames where the circus had been playing for a week. What an experience it proved to be, rehearsing in a circus ring, bent down over our music which was spread out at our feet on top of two or three inches of sawdust! Not surprisingly, the producer soon came running out of the control room to report that the TV monitor revealed us in a peculiar humped-back position. The only real solution, he said, was for us to rehearse the

*I recall big Jack Fallon, from London, Ontario, looking every inch a Canadian 'Mountie' in his stage uniform as he gazed down at me, saying, 'Oi vey, look at him already!'

number until we had it by memory, and this we were able to do in an unoccupied caravan. The going was tough, but we managed it by the time of the performance that Sunday evening.

While we took a break in the late afternoon I wandered around the circus with George Chisholm and the others, watching some of the performers putting the finishing touches to their acts. As the ringmaster ushered the elephants into the ring with his long staff, I noticed that the animals executed a kind of little skip as they passed him. I moved in closer to see if I could discover why they did this. To my horror I saw a steel pin, some five or six inches long, protruding from the end of the staff which was used to give each elephant a jab as it entered the ring. Angered by this, I remarked sharply how bloody clever the trainer thought he was, but he turned away, completely ignoring me.

It was thrilling, on the other hand, to watch a good-looking raven haired girl practising her act – swinging on a rope at least 70 feet above the ground and held only by a wriststrap. She was 18-year-old Carmen Rosaire who was born in Spain of an English father and who lived on the family farm in England when not working with the Circus.

Leaving the circus folk to their final preparations, we walked the short distance into the town for an early evening drink and some sandwiches. The band was not required until the second half of the programme and George left word where we could be found if needed. It was just as well he did, for one of the TV production team came later to the pub to tell us that the band would be required to play earlier than scheduled as there had been a tragic accident at the circus. Rehearsing her act one more time Carmen Rosaire somersaulted, looped and spun, just as we had seen her do that afternoon, 70 feet high in the air; but as she swung down and across the ring, her wriststrap snapped and she plunged 30 feet onto the sawdust, where she landed within a foot or two of 'Mr Pastry' (Richard Hearne). Sadly, she died in Kingston Hospital the following morning.

This tragedy brought to mind a particularly nasty road accident in which Tessa and I were involved some four years earlier and which could have had fatal consequences. On our way back from a holiday in Italy, we were in a head-on collision with another car outside Beauvais, near the French coast. The other driver, a doctor from the London Hospital, was driving on the wrong side of the road and I had simply no chance of avoiding him. Tessa lost four teeth in the crash and was unconscious for more than a quarter of an hour. I suffered injuries around both eyes.

A passing motorist took all of us to hospital where Tessa and I spent three nights (the doctor's wife was also injured) before we were able to continue our journey home, which we did by air to Lydd as our car, as well as the doctor's, was a write-off. The effects of Tessa's injuries are with her to this day, necessitating her regular attendance at the Eastman Dental Hospital.

While doing a date for George Chisholm at the BBC television studios in Shepherds Bush, just four days before Christmas 1960, I was given the sad news that my dear mother had passed away at Rokefield House, the Jewish Home for the Blind in Dorking, where she had been resident for some four years. Although not bed-ridden during her declining years, she had been completely blind. In accordance with her wishes we brought her home to rest beside my father in Marlow Road Cemetery, East Ham.

One day in April 1962 I received a call from Sam Norton, one of the directors of Boosey & Hawkes, who wanted me to play their make of clarinet for publicity purposes. I took the opportunity to tell them that I required a couple of extra keys – an articulated G sharp and a forked B flat – on their instrument, the same as on the one I was using, the one that is that Danny Polo had given me. Sam agreed and the job was put in hand at their factory.

Some four months later I was invited to the Boosey & Hawkes factory in Edgware. Among the five people present were the clarinet consultant, Jack Brymer, the chief tester, Eric McGavin, and Sam Norton who said with a chuckle as he handed me the clarinet – 'Have a blow!' The rich sound I obtained from this instrument gave me plenty of satisfaction and I really got a kick from playing it. Turning to Jack Brymer I murmured, 'It's like giving an audition!' 'You're doing fine,' he replied. Finally, I told Eric McGavin, 'This key is a little too long . . . this could be adjusted . . .' After the adjustments had been made Boosey & Hawkes presented me, on 3 September 1962, with a 'Symphony 10/10' B flat Clarinet which to this day I use alternately with Danny Polo's old instrument, now more than 50 years old.

During the run of Lionel Bart's *Blitz* at the Adelphi Theatre in The Strand, reed-player John Collier, on behalf of the jazz lovers in the pit orchestra, booked several seats at Ronnie Scott's Club in Soho so that we could go and hear that superb tenor sax man Stan Getz. On the night, from our front seats, it was noticeable that Stan was a little unsteady on his feet . . . maybe one drink too many! He kept whacking his crook and appealing to me to fix it. In front of the cream of the jazz world I was, to put it mildly, a little embarrassed as I muttered, 'Later, later, Stan.'

At interval time I joined Stan and his rhythm section in the bandroom under the pavement where he gave his boys farewell presents – he was making his last appearance at the club. Meanwhile I tested his tenor sax which was perfectly OK, blowing effortlessly . . . the way I've always played . . . I was delighted to have a chance of playing it. As Stan Getz presented pianist Stan Tracey with a cigarette lighter inscribed 'From Stan to Stan', Getz was on the point of tears – as well he might have been for he had given Tracey a hard time with his 'not like that, play it like this' routine.

It was at Ronnie Scott's that I heard Stan Getz 'live' for the first time. It was a memorable occasion for me. He played with an uncommon blend of drive and relaxation. His playing of ballad numbers was masterly. Afterwards, as John Collier and I climbed the stairs to the street, John pondered: 'I wonder what kind of mouthpiece he uses.' As I suggested that it was a five lay, a voice behind us chipped in, 'It's a five star Meyer.' Turning round we saw that the voice belonged to Stan Getz himself. 'It sounds great,' I commented, speaking to Stan for the first time in my life. A few moments later he asked if I could get him the telephone number of a lovely looking young Indian girl who was also on the point of leaving the club. It turned out, however, that she was just a keen jazz lover and not interested in any fooling around. 'Sorry, Stan,' I grinned. 'You're out of luck this time – but will you have lunch with me tomorrow?' He declined, though he gave me his telephone number so that we might arrange a date later on. I did ring him several times but got no reply. Nevertheless, during our short chat I learned that he was very nearly born in the East End of London, his mother arriving in the United States only a short while before he turned up! Stan also told me that as a result of playing alongside so many 'greats', such as Ben Webster, Coleman Hawkins and Lester Young, a little of their talent had rubbed off onto him over the years. He laughed when I observed, 'Who could have such luck!' During our conversation I found him to be a sociable sort of fellow: Ronnie Scott, on the other hand, found Stan not always so easy to deal with.

27 'Somewhere at Sea'

During the second half of the 1960s work for the jazz and dance band musician was not at all plentiful due to the arrival of the guitar dominated groups who virtually took over the popular music scene. I had no desire to have a permanent job playing in the pit orchestras of London shows; but I was happy enough to deputise, combining this with gigs for both Harry Kahn and Tommy Kinsman.

In his early days Harry Kahn was pianist/arranger for Joe Loss. His brothers Dave and Alfie were also musicians, the former a trumpet player, the latter a tenor saxophonist and clarinettist. Alfie served in Bomber Command during World War II and when his plane was shot down he was the sole survivor. Telling me about what must have been a terrifying experience, Alfie jokingly added that it had knocked him sensible!

One day in the summer of 1971 Harry Kahn telephoned me with the news that he had secured an engagement for the band to play on the liner *Oronsay* for a 15-day Mediterranean cruise. The offer was very attractive for wives were to be included and we were promised first-class accommodation and given officer status. Remembering how seasick I had been when crossing to Dublin and to France with Ambrose and Geraldo, my feelings were somewhat mixed: I recalled the time when I had heeded the advice of Sam Browne and Joe Brannelly on the crossing to France and taken a large brandy, only to end up vomiting violently in the toilet! On the other hand, it was always a pleasure to work with Harry Kahn's well-organised outfit and I felt that Tessa would find the sea air beneficial. In the event, I wasn't seasick – but she was!

We embarked on 26 September with a six-piece lineup – Harry leading on piano, with Neil Fullerton (t); Harry Klein (bar); Les Collins (b); Brian Emney (d); myself on clarinet and tenor, and that wonderful trouper Lynn Collins (no relation of Les) supplying the vocals. Except when the ship was in port, we played music for dancing every night in the ballroom for about an hour and a half. Harry Kahn's music library was extensive and included not only the popular tunes of the day but many old standards as well, the more modern composers – Bacharach, Sondheim, Mancini and The Beatles for example – alongside many of those from former days such as Gershwin, Berlin, Kern, Porter, Rodgers and Harry Warren. Our girl singer had plenty of opportunity to demonstrate her lovely voice, besides showing what other talents as an entertainer she possessed.

When we went ashore at Athens Tessa and I met Professor Garby, a college lecturer and the author of two books on marine engineering. As animal lovers we thought ourselves fortunate to meet him, for he owned ten acres of land a few miles from Athens which he had developed into an animal sanctuary. Although he spoke with an accent we were surprised to learn that he was in fact English but had lived in Greece since being 'demobbed' and had spoken his native tongue so little that he had automatically acquired a foreign accent when he did use it. While we were there he invited us to a Wine Festival at which, after the first glass had been paid for, all further drinks were free. To remind us that the world is indeed small we met BBC producer Johnnie Stewart's secretary at the Festival.

In Malta the band, together with wives and entertainers from the ship, enjoyed a night out at the luxurious Corinthian Palace where, as part of the cabaret a stunning young Parisian girl singer required a 'stooge' for her act. The boys from the band did their best to encourage me to go up – their 'best' being to carry me there bodily! Once on stage I decided to make the most of it. The girl wore a beautiful dress, laced at the front to reveal an attractive cleavage. For a joke I looked down with the observation, 'That's a nice letter-box – post early for Christmas!' 'You naughty boy,' she whispered; to which I replied, 'Watch it – my wife's down there and she's a weight lifter!' I got another laugh when I lifted my trouser leg and pretended to scratch – a little gesture I borrowed from Les Carew who used it on the Ambrose stage shows. 'Are you a comedian?' the girl asked me. 'No, I'm Jewish,' I cracked back. At the end of the act she invited me to join her later for a drink. However, when I returned to our table where Tessa, O'Donnell, the ship's officer in charge of accommodation, and his girl friend were sitting, the management presented me with two bottles of wine.

It was a happy and boisterous party that boarded the ferry to take us back to the *Oronsay* in the early hours of the morning, and, with the extra bottles of wine taking effect, I found myself asking the skipper if I could take the wheel. He allowed me to do so until we got close to the ship – almost too close, for the helmsman had to grab the wheel quickly to avoid an 'incident', much to everyone's relief. The four of us rounded off the night, or what was left of it, in O'Donnell's cabin where he had a large collection of LPs and an even larger cabinet of drinks.

Our first meeting with O'Donnell had not been all that agreeable: when the P&O office allowed the band to board the ship the night before we were to sail, we had to summon O'Donnell from his bed to unlock our cabins. Lynn Collins, who appeared to be in a hurry, said to him in a none too friendly tone of voice, 'I'm the vocalist in the band,' to which O'Donnell growled sleepily, 'Congratulations!' We met up with him a few times on the various cruises, and on one occasion, over a drink in his cabin, he and I went into one of those 'where-do-you-come-from' routines. After I told him that, prior to moving to Kenton, I had lived for 27 years in Kilburn (NW6), he slightly amazed me by saying, 'I know that part well – I used to drive a No 28 bus through that area!' I remarked, 'I knew there was a hidden talent in you somewhere . . . give me another drink.' Maybe I should have said, 'Congratulations'!

The fun on the cruise was never-ending, with plenty of swimming, gala nights, dancing and making new friends, attending Masonic parties and the Captain's cocktail parties. One fellow, well over six feet tall, was standing beside me on deck one afternoon watching the antics of some dolphins through his binoculars. I looked up (that's the story of my life!), and as he gazed down I asked him, 'May I have a look, please?' 'OK,' he replied, and as we chatted it occurred to me, not for the first time, how small the world really is, for he and his wife, Denise, lived quite near to us in Kenton. His name was Derek Chester; he had once been a policeman and was also something of a musician, having at one time had lessons on the clarinet from Alfie Kahn. We remain friends to this day.

With a few hours to spend in Palma, Tessa and I took the opportunity – as millions have done before and since – to visit the magnificent thirteenth century Gothic cathedral which dominates the bay. As I looked at the row of suggestion boxes, in almost every language, on one of its walls, I was sorely tempted to request one in Yiddish!

28   A Royal Favourite

In the late 1960s Ralph Goldsmith 'fixed' me for numerous gigs with Tommy Kinsman, the Queen Mother's favourite society bandleader. He became so, apparently, because whenever his band was engaged for any function at which the Queen Mother was present, Tommy always seemed to anticipate when she was about to take the floor, and would signal to the boys to play her favourite dance music – the Viennese waltz.

Tommy, whose youthful looks belied his years in the days when I was associated with him, was born in Liverpool and began his musical career playing the banjo before taking up the saxophone. For radio and recording sessions he generally used a 13-piece orchestra of five reeds, four brass and four rhythm, but tended to reduce the personnel for gigs, with himself fronting the band but seldom playing his saxophone.

I had been used to playing sessions for many years, where the band parts had been arranged, so this work was strange to me. Indeed, many session men do not take on gigs, i.e. where there are no arrangements so that improvisation and a sound memory are essential. I was determined to become a good gigster, and with a combination of patience on Tommy's part and guidance from Len Pacey, the accordion player, I became well versed in the current numbers of the time. Harry Rainer, who had been one of the earliest pianists to play for Mrs Kate Meyrick at the '43 Club in Gerrard Street, being a natural 'jazzer' was also a considerable help to me, as well as being a cornerstone of the Kinsman band.

I found the experience of playing these gigs both pleasurable and stimulating. The band played at a number of interesting places, such as Blenheim Palace, Badminton, the Royal Naval College, the Royal College of Physicians, Lancaster House, the Guildhall and the Dutch and Belgian embassies. The first time I played for Tommy at Blenheim Palace the band was shown the bedroom where Sir Winston Churchill slept when he was a child, and there was a glass case containing a lock of his hair. The old fashioned fireplace with its magnificent brass fender was most impressive. We may not have been the best band in the world, but we certainly played in the best places!

There was one date at the Dorchester Hotel when Michael Bentine, one time fourth member of the Goons, was part of the cabaret. He began his act, as I had so often seen him do during warmups for 'The Goon Show' before a studio audience, announcing in a slightly high-pitched voice and under a huge mop of black hair – 'Ladies and Gentlemen: some of you may be under the impression that I am wearing a wig – well, I am!' So saying, he removed the wig to reveal his own – just as huge – thick mop of hair . . . then slumped to the floor. The patrons roared with laughter, but, as the applause died away, the inert figure of Michael Bentine continued lying on the floor. There was a hush as he was carried away, though few among the audience realised that he had suffered a blackout.

On another date with Tommy at the Dorchester we provided music for the Lancastrians' Ball, hosted by impressario and former bandleader Jack Hylton. To my knowledge Jack rarely slept regularly and on this particular night I came across him taking a nap in the hotel lounge. I walked quietly up to him and whispered in his ear, 'Are you working New Year's Eve?' As he opened one eye and gazed wearily up at me, I added: 'Are you feeling all right, Jack?' 'Yes,' he replied with a grin; 'I have insomnia and I'm trying to sleep it off.'

Arriving one night for a Tommy Kinsman gig at the Hyde Park Hotel, the manager, Mr Osbourne, gave me a glance of recognition. I returned his glance and smiled at him; then I realised that he was a familiar face from the past. When we left the bandstand for the interval, he was standing nearby. He beckoned me to go behind the screen where he had his own table. 'Hullo, Billy,' he said. 'It's been years, hasn't it?' It had certainly been almost 40 years since our last meeting, for at the May Fair Hotel in 1932 he had been the young 'commie' boy (the lowest form of restaurant life, clearing tables, running errands etc) who used to keep the band supplied with iced water, such a thirsty bunch we were! Now he asked me to join him for a glass of wine at his private table where we reminisced until it was time for me to return to the bandstand.

At the same hotel one evening, on another date with Tommy, I came almost face to face with a very tall, elderly and elegant gentleman who was on the point of leaving the ballroom. As I held open the big heavy glass doors for him, he beamed at me and said, 'Thank you, you're a good boy.' Walking back into the ballroom I reflected on those words, which were the exact ones used so often by Ambrose when he was pleased with one of his 'boys'. This time, however, they were spoken by King Haakon of Norway, who, during the German occupation of his country during World War II, always wore the Star of David on his breast in defiance of the Nazis.

In August 1973 there was a very unusual gig when Tommy was asked to play at a party in Estorial in Portugal. The hosts were a prominent Portuguese doctor and his Irish born wife. Eight of us flew to Lisbon and stayed in a four-star hotel for three days the overall cost of which came to £2000. The doctor's villa was imposing to say the least, with magnificent gardens, swimming pool, flower ponds, and floodlighting. The occasion must have been an extremely important anniversary or celebration – or perhaps the wife was just a fan of our dapper leader. We were regally treated, with the doctor sending a car to the hotel on the evening of the party to take us to the villa; but as there wasn't room for all of us, Tommy hired a taxi. We played on the terrace for dancing in the open air until 4am and then as the host and hostess thanked each one of individually, Tommy asked the doctor for that taxi fare!

Having found playing on the P&O line 'a piece of cake', I persuaded Tommy

Kinsman to contact a friend of his who was a director of the Union Castle line, to ask him to use his influence to obtain work for the band on their cruise liners. The result was trips on the *Reina del Mar* to the northern capitals – Bergen, Copenhagen, Stockholm and Leningrad – and also to the West Indies. One of the longest cruises was to South Africa on the *Windsor Castle*, flagship of the Union Castle line.

When the *Windsor Castle* docked at Durban, Tessa and I visited David Godfrey, brother of the late Isadore Godfrey, for many years conductor of the D'Oyly Carte Opera Company. This was only the second time that we had met David since our wedding when he had entertained our guests with his particular brand of humour.

On the journey to Barbados in the mid-1970s the *Reina del Mar* received a Mayday call from a small British cargo ship, and we sailed off-course for some 200 miles to the assistance of a case of suspected appendicitis. Amid cheers from the passengers a lad of 18 was hoisted on board by a crane, in a stretcher. Apart from receiving the medical attention he so urgently needed, he also received a sum of £200 which had been raised from a collection among the passengers. We learned later that he had been successfully operated on.

It was on that trip that Tommy Kinsman and his Japanese girl friend Tomoko were taking an afternoon stroll in Antigua when, having strayed from the main highways, they were held up at gun point by two thugs. Tomoko urged Tommy not to part with his money, but as he later told us, he thought it was much better to lose his money than his life! Back on the *Reina del Mar* Tommy made his way to the bar where the barman, noticing his hands shaking, gave him a couple of large brandies. Tommy's hands stopped shaking after the drinks – as they always did, he told me, for that was the effect liquor had on the Parkinson's Disease from which he suffered.*

*Early in 1982 Tommy retired and left England with Tomoko to live in Marbella on the Spanish Costa del Sol. We corresponded from time to time and in February 1984 Tommy sent me a photograph which appears in this book. He is seen fronting his band at the Hyde Park Hotel in 1954, on the occasion of the Balaclava Ball, held to mark the centenary of the Charge of the Light Brigade. In his accompanying letter he wrote that many of the Royal Family attended the ball. A month later, José Carroll, who was the singer when I was in the band on the *Reina del Mar*, telephoned me to give me the sad news that Tommy died on 15 March at a clinic in Málaga, where he had been taken after suffering a second stroke at his Marbella home.

29 Absent Friends and 'Autumn Leaves'

Saturday 12 June 1971 was a sad day for me –for it was the day on which saxophonist Harry Smith telephoned me the news of Ambrose's sudden death. Harry had heard over the radio that 'Ammy' had collapsed in a TV studio in Leeds the previous night and had died in the ambulance on the way to hospital. I had not seen him for some time, but the last occasion was quite clear in my memory. Stanley Black and I had met him at the TV studios in Lime Grove, where he was accompanied by his singing protégéé Kathy Kirby and we were left in no doubt that he was delighted to meet two of his former 'boys' once again.

Early on the Sunday morning a distressed Joe Jeannette telephoned to tell me what I of course knew already. 'Billy,' he asked, 'what are we going to do about the funeral?' I was not quite sure what he had in mind, until he added: 'We should let the boys know.' I told him I would call the Burial Society immediately, and on doing so was informed that the body was being brought to London for burial at Bushey Cemetery on the following day (Monday) at 11.30 am. Joe and I at once arranged to telephone certain of the 'boys', asking each one to ring another, and in this way we managed to contact 30 or more of Ambrose's former musicians. I recall that I first contacted Tommy McQuater, asking him to inform George Chisholm and then I spoke to Stanley Black, who was able to postpone a pressing appointment so that he could pay his last respects.

At Bushey Cemetery that Monday morning about 30 of Ambrose's 'boys' attended the service, including, apart from those already mentioned, Joe Brannelly, Sid Simone, Reg Leopold and Kenny Baker. Kathy Kirby and Joan Linton were also present, but there was only one relative, a nephew who was a stranger to all of us. The Reverend who conducted the service had obviously not been properly briefed or had not troubled to brief himself, for in his address the best he could manage was a most inadequate: 'Mr Ambrose was well known on the wireless.'

Although I knew Bert Ambrose for 40 years, never once did I call him 'Ammy'. At first, as I have said, I addressed him as 'Mr Ambrose'. It was quite some time before I called him 'Bert' – but never 'Ammy'. A most loveable man was 'Mr Ambrose'.

After the funeral Tessa and I invited Joe Jeannette and his wife, Mabel, to lunch at our home in Kenton where Joe and I reminisced at length, for we were Bert's longest serving musicians. Joe expressed his thought on Ambrose in a letter he wrote to me two days after the funeral –

116

'. . . Many of us will be eternally grateful to the man we said goodbye to on Monday – the association with him made it possible for some of us to make a very decent living. For others, the chance he gave them really put them on the map – a great pity they were not there at the end. Maybe they could not make it. It *was* rather hurried . . .'

In the early 1970s, between work on the cruise liners, *Oronsay*, *Oriana* and *Orsova*, my freelance jobs included a series of broadcasts with Sid Phillips's band. By this time Sid had been a close friend for 40 years and a colleague for a good part of the time. Not only had we shared 'digs' when touring with Ambrose but had gone around together in the tough areas of Liverpool and Glasgow, where I always felt safe in his company. We talked about music at great length over the years and I learned a lot from him. Basically he was a modest man – although many musicians might not agree with me – as I once found when commenting how effective his arrangement of the verse of *Limehouse Blues* was. Sid became quite bashful! He played neat, expert and razzle-dazzle clarinet, never failing to capture the sound to suit a particular situation, as he so frequently demonstrated on those famous Saturday night Ambrose broadcasts.

Sid's talented musical career, for which he gave up one in medicine, has been well documented; but he was a man of many parts. When the Ambrose orchestra played the Holborn Empire in November 1935, young Johnny Brown, the professional boxer, came to our dressing room a number of times and, as I looked on in admiration, sparred a couple of rounds with Sid, who had been an Amateur Boxing Association Champion in his day. He was also a very good cricketer who, like his brother Woolf, had played for the Middlesex County 2nd XI. In addition he was a multi-linguist who spoke French, Dutch, German, Spanish and Italian; and as if those were not enough talents for one man, Sid was adept with brush and canvas, besides being something of an inventor! During World War II he served in RAF Intelligence where no doubt his linguistic ability was of great value.

As if that was not all, he was a bit of a joker as well. There was that time when he tried to 'lumber' me by putting two blank bars . . . *ad lib* lead in to solo from the key of F to A (tenor pitch) in his arrangement of *Streamline Strut*. With a bit of quick thinking on the recording session, I think I managed it well – as the record shows. Such was the keenness in the Ambrose orchestra.

I well remember my last date with Sid's band – an engagement near Birmingham on 1 March 1973 with Sid's son Simon playing drums. At only 16 years of age the boy was an outstanding prospect, to whom no kinds of rhythm posed any problems.

I was glad that, to and from that date, I sat beside Sid on the coach and enjoyed chatting over days gone by, for within three months he suffered a heart attack and died on 25 May at St Peter's Hospital, Chertsey, Surrey. I attended his funeral at the Hoop Lane Crematorium, Golders Green. Among the mourners from the musical profession were Tommy McQuater, Arthur Coppersmith, Harry Smith and Sid's trumpeter from the mid-1950s, Kenny Ball, who was overcome with emotion. But Sid had his last wish: his sister Rose told me that it was always his wish to be cremated.

One morning in early November 1976, a man's voice asked over the telephone: 'Are you Billy Amstell, the clarinet player?' When I informed him that I was and asked how I could help him, he replied by asking if I knew the tune *Autumn Leaves*? Replying that I did, he then posed yet another question – 'Would you play it at my wife's funeral, at the side of her grave?' I had the feeling that this must be a 'lumber' in the worse possible taste. However, giving the voice the benefit of the doubt, I replied, somewhat cautiously, that I might be willing to do so, whereupon he asked how much it would cost. In my experience such a musical request was unparalleled and I had no idea what to charge. 'Would £15 do?' he asked. I was still not convinced that it was a serious proposition, so to draw him out into the open, I suggested that he should call to see me that afternoon. Somewhat to my surprise, he arrived as arranged, and introducing himself as Denis Parker placed £15 on the table, saying, 'Is that enough?' Despite the fact that I indicted that it was quite enough, he deposited a further £10 on the table and pressed me to accept it. He told me what time to be at West Harrow Cemetery on the following morning. I was so taken aback by the nature of the job that I completely forgot to ask him from whom, or from where, he had obtained my name and telephone number. Later on I concluded that he must have read a brief profile of my career in music which had appeared in the Harrow–Wembley Independent Newspaper a few weeks previously.

The next morning I arrived at the cemetery with my clarinet and after the service joined the gathering on the slow walk to the grave for the burial of Denis Parker's wife, Angela, a Chinese girl of only 21 years who had been a nurse at the Middlesex Hospital and had died in childbirth. As the coffin was lowered into the grave I commenced playing *Autumn Leaves* . . . Then we dispersed and Parker thanked me for playing what had been his wife's favourite tune.

I was reminded of that sorrowful occasion some two years later when 'Peanuts' Hucko played the tune at the Wembley Conference Centre as a guest with the Syd Lawrence Orchestra for the annual Glenn Miller Memorial Concert. The song seemed to haunt me. In December 1981 Bert Wilcox, the Pathfinders Social Functions Officer, invited me to the Pathfinders Ball at the Savoy Hotel where my colleague from Harry Kahn's outfit, Les Collins, led the band that night. I was asked to play the clarinet and after being introduced by the radio and TV entertainer, Harold Bernes, I played three numbers from the centre of the floor, one of which was *Autumn Leaves*, unaccompanied, as requested by Bert Wilcox, a veteran of 56 operational flights.

The following November my five-piece band recorded eight titles for the Radio 2 programme 'You and the Night and the Music', one of the titles being (inevitably) *Autumn Leaves*. My friend Norman Joyce, the clarinettist, has paid me the compliment of playing some of my compositions in recent years with the Spa Orchestra led by Max Jaffa at Scarborough during the summer season. In May 1983 I scored *Autumn Leaves* for Norman, who features it . . . unaccompanied.

30 'Way Down Yonder in New Orleans'

Towards the end of the summer of 1978, Hughie Slavin, Assistant Head of Entertainment at the P&O line telephoned me with an invitation to play on board their flagship, the *Canberra*, on her first visit to New Orleans. I was flattered when he added that, having heard I had been made an Honorary Citizen of New Orleans for my services to jazz over a period of more than 50 years, he thought it appropriate that I be given the chance to travel there on the *Canberra*'s cruise to the American Deep South. As the invitation also included Tessa I was delighted to accept the opportunity to see the city which had, on 22 March that year, made me an Honorary Citizen. The certificate confirming that I had been awarded the honour was accompanied by a Key to the City, both of which had been sent to me by the Mayor, to whom I wrote that I anticipated being in the city by the middle of November and would telephone him on my arrival. Hughie Slavin, a Glaswegian and a drummer of note in his day, arranged for me to play with Jack Nathan's group, which comprised Jack on piano plus bass and drums. Among the host of other entertainers on board were Ray Davies and the Button Down Brass, classical pianist Walter Landauer, together with antiques expert Arthur Negus and gardening authority Percy Thrower.

The *Canberra*, 45,000 tons of truly magnificent ship, sailed from Southampton on 4 November, stopping off some six days later in Bermuda. Twenty-four hours later we were on our way to Port Everglades, Miami, America's great holiday playground where the weather seems warm all the year round. After an all too brief stay there we set off for the two day journey to New Orleans, where jazz is everywhere, especially in the clubs along Bourbon Street and in Jackson Square and where the cosmopolitan mixture of cultures – French, Spanish, Italian, Creole and Negro – pervades everything from the buildings to the food.

The night before we arrived the ship's resident vocalist and Master of Ceremonies, Ray Merrell, who must have been tipped off by Hughie Slavin that I was to meet the Mayor, hauled me out onto the ballroom floor during the cabaret time and introduced me to the passengers as having come on the cruise 'to help Jack Nathan out' (nothing could have been further from the truth) and adding that I had played with all the famous British dance bands of the past. 'Tell us just what bands you have played with, Billy,' he cued me. 'Well,' I replied, 'I played with Roy Fox when the Monseigneur Restaurant opened in May 1931 (I could here the "Ohs" from the older passengers); then I joined Ambrose at the May Fair Hotel, remaining with him for nine years until I enlisted in the RAF. Following my discharge I played with Geraldo – do you want any more?' He nodded, so I

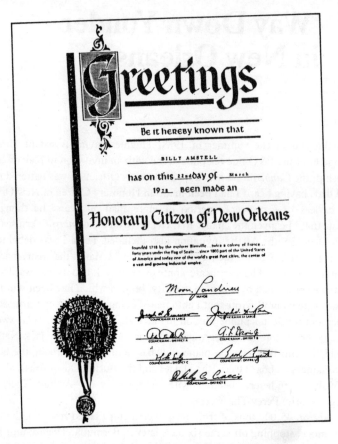

Greetings

Be it hereby known that

BILLY AMSTELL

has on this 22nd day of March 19 72 been made an

Honorary Citizen of New Orleans

founded 1718 by the explorer Bienville . . . twice a colony of France . .
forty years under the flag of Spain . . . since 1803 part of the United States
of America and today one of the world's great Port cities, the center of
a vast and growing industrial empire.

continued: 'Ambrose again, then there was a short spell of six and a half years with Stanley Black . . . Geoff Love . . Eric Robinson – and if you want any more than that it'll cost you a bottle of whisky!' 'Thanks,' Ray said hastily. 'Give Billy a big hand!'

When we docked in New Orleans I met Nick Adams, the Chief of Port Police, who was most helpful when I asked to be directed to a telephone so that I could call the Mayor's office. Nick took me to a telephone and made sure that I had a 'dime' while my eyes fixed on the metal badge of office which he wore. 'You can't have that,' he insisted. Needless to say, I do have it today as part of my collection. During that all too short visit we met Nick's wife and were asked to visit them again, but I had to say that it was not as if we lived 'just around the corner'. However, we do correspond.

The following afternoon I met Ernest N. Morial, the Mayor, at City Hall, and took tea with him in his office where he and his staff were most courteous. Also, it seemed to be something of a novelty for them to hear my English accent – little did they know I was a Cockney!

Just before we left New Orleans I wanted to give Nick Adams a drink. As I knew he was on duty I filled a ginger ale bottle with whisky – I didn't want to be seen leaving the ship carrying a large bottle of spirits – and descended the gangway. Greeting Nick I handed him what looked like a bottle of ginger ale and said, 'Have a drink, Nick.' Giving me an incredulous look, he replied: 'I never touch THAT stuff!' 'Go on, try it, it's special,' I told him. He accepted the bottle and disappeared round the side of one of the dock buildings. He returned a couple of minutes later, laughing heartily, and bellowed: 'That's the greatest ginger ale I've ever tasted!'

That night Tessa and I called in for a drink at the Hilton Hotel, which possesses one of the largest circular bars that I have ever seen. Very dimly lit – possibly to protect one's eyes from the price list! – I couldn't make out where the music was coming from until I spotted the bandstand. Even then I had difficulty in seeing the excellent coloured pianist who was giving out with many of the old standards.

Our last port of call before setting out on the return journey was Charleston, a fine old town built in the days of King Cotton and surrounded by numerous splendid gardens. Our arrival was greeted with the students' band from the local High School, playing *Charleston* – what else? Taking their youthfulness into consideration, they played really well. As I stood in the market place, situated just beyond the Customs building, I realised that I was on the spot where, only a little more than 100 years ago, slaves had been bought and sold.

In the *Canberra*'s brochure it is stated that the second oldest synagogue in the USA is in Charleston. Tessa and I managed to locate it, but to our astonishment we were unable to gain admittance: the 'ever open door' of any place of worship is, in this case, kept locked during the hours of darkness, except for prayers and services. The coloured caretaker told us that he was unable to open the *shul* for us because of the security regulations in force – alas, a sign of the times in which we live.

At some point on a cruise it is the custom to get all the bands together for a big 'jazz up'. Following a particularly hefty 'jam session' with the Button Down Brass and the House Bands of Jack Duff and 'Sounds Around' one night, I returned to our table, clarinet in hand, to be complimented by Commodore F. B. Woolley, RD, RNR, who was sitting nearby. Thanking him, I added – 'If I let you play my clarinet will you let me drive your ship?' He was kind enough to have a drink sent up to toast his health, and I was happy to settle for that.

The *Canberra* sailed home via the Spanish port of Vigo, with its narrow streets and little squares dating from medieval times, and reached Southampton after a wonderful 26 days working holiday.

The cruises which began with the *Oronsay* in 1971 ended for me with the *Canberra* at the end of 1978. In all I had made 12 cruises. One ship that I have not so far mentioned was the *Orsova*, playing with Harry Kahn. I count myself lucky that I was able to take my wife with me every time, enjoying first class travel on each ship.

Perhaps the funniest incident involving a dance band musician on a cruise liner concerned Sid Heiger, my former RAF dance band drummer. On any cruise there are a number of ladies travelling alone – spinsters, widows, divorcées, some of whom may be just looking for company, some for a shipboard romance, others for a passing sexual encounter. Playing for the Geraldo office on the *Queen Mary*, Sid met up with one of the latter who invited him to her cabin, ostensibly for a couple of drinks. Sid's crowning glory was certainly never his hair – to have described him as a 'Brylcream boy' in his RAF days would have been to flatter him beyond any call of duty. Lack of hair never seemed to bother Sid, except for his work on the cruise liners. For this he acquired a toupee, in order to look more presentable – or so he said. One drink with this lady led to another and eventually to their making love. At a critical moment she ran her fingers through Sid's 'hair', only for the toupee to come away in her hand! Love flew out of the porthole as Sid donned his trousers and made a rapid and embarrassed exit.

There was a rather frightening experience for some on board the *Orsova* one night as we headed out into the Atlantic at the end of September 1973. The Harry Kahn band and the ship's other entertainers were in the dining saloon when one of the portholes nearest to where the members of the band and their wives were sitting suddenly blew out during a heavy storm. For several minutes some panic ensued while musicians and wives were thoroughly drenched. As the heavy seas lashed up with frightening ferocity, Neil Fullerton's wife Mary became almost hysterical. Tessa and I, however, were in our cabin where I was recovering from an upset stomach, so we missed out on all the excitement – and a total soaking, for we were told later that the main force of the water had been directed toward the seats we usually occupied.

Soon after the trip on the *Orsova* I was asked to do a recording session with my band for Decca. For that job I fixed the following personnel: Duncan Campbell (t); Peter Hodge (tbn); Brian Lemon (p); Geoff Lofts (d); Ron Black (b); with myself on clarinet. We played that old favourite from the 1920s, *What do you Want to Make those Eyes at Me for?*. We were told that a vocal would be added on the second chorus, so I played a little background clarinet. For the other side of the 'single' the number was *Lucy*, the vocal this time being on the first chorus. When we had finished the engineers added the vocals, which were by Terry Venables, the former Chelsea and 'Spurs midfield footballer, currently with Queen's Park Rangers. Terry was supported by a vocal group.

When I returned from the cruise to the Northern capitals I learned that the 'A' side had been played nearly 20 times on the air and had almost got into the charts. Having listened to the test pressings before I left, I thought it might become a hit because I found the vocals so inadequate! The record was also promoted on television when Terry Venables, the Billy Amstell Jazz Band (according to the credit on the record label) and the vocal group, were given a spot on the Russell Harty Show with the QPR first team squad in the studio audience. The star of the show that night, however, at least so far as the band was concerned, was Terry Venables' most beautiful looking wife in a closeup shot. I was amazed that she had not been 'discovered' instead of Terry, whose decision not to continue as a professional singer was, I am sure, a wise one!

31 Reunion with 'Peanuts' Hucko

Angela Morley, who composed and scored the music for *The Slipper and the Rose* and *Watership Down*, and her companion Christine, were having tea with Tessa and I one afternoon in June 1978, when she mentioned that 'Peanuts' Hucko was back in England playing the clubs and giving concerts. Thirty-four years had passed since he and I last met, so when I learned that he was playing at Thatchers Hotel in East Horsley near Guildford, Tessa and I motored there to find the place crammed with about 200 fans and jazz enthusiasts, most of whom had come to listen rather than dance.

As we walked to the bar I spotted 'Peanuts'. Sneaking up behind him I whispered in his ear, 'Benny Goodman said you play out of tune!' He turned round in surprise, then recognising me he nearly crushed my ribs with an affectionate hug. While he was over here I arranged for him to be shown over the Boosey & Hawkes factory in Edgware to try out one of their instruments. David James, their chief clarinet tester, kindly invited us to a reception lunch, during which our visitor told us something about his background. He revealed that in the States he had studied with the British born clarinettist Reginald Kell, and that when he joined the school band and took up the saxophone as a young lad, he appeared so small beside his instrument that he was immediately given the nickname 'Peanuts'.

He and his charming wife Louise Tobin – they first met when they were both with Benny Goodman (she as a singer) – then visited our home in Kenton. Seeing my open instrument case in the music room, 'Peanuts' became interested in my almost wornout old clarinet. I showed him the Selmer HS Double Star mouthpiece he had given me in 1944, and after having a 'blow' he remarked, 'That's terrible!' 'Is that why you gave it to me?' I asked him. He promised that he had an excellent one for me this time. As good as his word, he gave me a glass mouthpiece made by a friend of his in the States. It really is first class and I never tire of using it. Furthermore, it has solved the problem whether or not I should buy another clarinet! Telephoning me later he asked what I thought of the mouthpiece, to which I replied, 'It's fine, you saved my life!' 'Well then, 'Peanuts' said, 'use it in good health, Billy.' His own health at the time was not at all good. He was suffering a lot of pain in the lower spine, and back in the US he underwent a five and a half hour successful operation, which enabled him to return to England that December for the 1978 Glenn Miller Memorial Concert at the Wembley Conference Centre, compered by Alan Dell. He invited Tessa and I to the concert where he was guesting with the Syd Lawrence Orchestra. From the stage he recalled the time when he and I were in the Services, announcing: 'From one Sergeant to another, here's a little number for my friend Billy Amstell, who is in the audience tonight – *Stealin' Apples*' I was totally bowled over.

A couple of years later Tessa and I were at the annual meeting of the Glenn Miller Music Society at the Shaftesbury Hotel in London, where 'Peanuts' and trombonist Nat Peck were the guests of honour. Nat, one of Glenn Miller's original members, was the good-looking fellow who sat at the extreme end of the orchestra. I had previously told 'Peanuts' about the metal badge that Glenn Miller had given me and which I had treasured for 36 years. That day I got the feeling that he might like to have it as a souvenir. We arrived at the meeting to be greeted by Louise, who then beckoned to her husband and Nat as they stood on the bandstand chatting over old times. I gave 'Peanuts' the badge, which he accepted with some emotion; and holding it high in the air, made off towards the bandstand. It was rather funny to see a number of cameras click into action taking pictures of a hand holding a badge! 'Peanuts' told the fans that Glenn had given the badge to me in 1944, and now, all those years later, I had passed it on to him; whereupon the audience, to my amazement, went frantic with joy.

The meeting was quite informal, with people of all ages and from all walks of life socialising together. I had a drink at the bar with 'Peanuts' and Nat during the interval, after which they returned to the bandstand to thank me publicly for my gesture and my presence. The longer the meeting went on, the more convivial did it become. I remember a youngster coming up to me to express his appreciation of my playing in the orchestras of Ambrose and Geraldo. 'That was a very long time ago,' I said to him. 'How old are you?' When he told me he was 19, I asked him: 'How is it that you know about those bands of the distant past?' 'My father has all the records,' he replied. 'Can't win, can I?' I muttered.

Less than three months later 'Peanuts' wrote to me from his home in Sherman Oaks, California, partly to let met know that he would be touring England in May 1981 with the Pied Piper Quintet. When the time came I went along to the Pizza Restaurant in Dean Street, Soho; it was crowded with jazz fans who had come to hear 'Peanuts' and the Quintet, which also featured Peter Appleyard on vibes. On another occasion 'Peanuts' introduced me to Billy Butterfield, the trumpet player who came to the fore with the Bob Crosby orchestra in 1937, before playing with many of the 'greats', including Benny Goodman, Artie Shaw, Lester Young, Yank Lawson and Bob Haggart. Billy told me that he had played violin, bass and trombone before switching to trumpet and later flügelhorn.

'Peanuts' visited England again in September 1984, this time with drummer Ray McKinley and former Miller trumpeter Zeke Zarchy to record a memorial programme with the 3rd USAF Band, commemorating the fortieth anniversary of Glenn Miller's passing. This re-creation of one of Glenn Miller's wartime concerts was hosted by Ann Shelton at RAF Lakenhall in Suffolk and was shown on BBC television in December. 'Peanuts' telephoned me on his arrival in England, and I asked him how things were with him. He said he felt tired and the going was getting tougher all the time. 'How old are you?' I asked him. 'Sixty-six,' he answered. 'So, I'm seven years older than you.' 'You always were,' he replied.

32 Session After Midnight

In the Spring of 1980 Tessa and I received an invitation to the 'Memory Lane' meeting in the Ambassador Suite of the Shaftesbury Hotel in London. Bert Wilcox, the organiser, when sending out the tickets wrote '. . . you are welcome to join in the 'jam' session if you wish . . .' So on 17 May I arrived at the Shaftesbury Hotel with my clarinet. The Ambassador Suite was packed with nearly 250 people, among them some of the readers and writers for the magazine *Memory Lane*, which devotes its pages to the popular music of the 1920s, 1930s and 1940s, with special emphasis on the musicians and vocalists of the period. How good it was to see familiar faces from the past – Billy Munn, Joe Crossman, Harry Gold, Joe Daniels, Alfie Noakes, Ivor Mairants and Tiny Winters, all musicians I had played with during my career. Then there were the vocalists – Ann Lenner, Helen Raymond, Pat Hyde, Hughie Diamond and Ken Crossley. Lew Stone's widow, Joyce, was also present, as was Chris Ellis of World Records who has compiled and produced so many LPs of music of the period.

ITN cameraman Don Thompson showed his excellent 30-minute film documentary on Sam Browne, which has been televised in New Zealand but not in this country. It was a most happy party during which I played clarinet with Billy Munn on piano, Joe Daniels at the drums and Hughie Diamond taking the vocals, and many other artistes present did a spot before the night was over.

The following day Bert Wilcox telephoned me to ask: 'How would you like to make a jazz album with your band for my company, Zodiac Records?' When I had recovered from the shock I invited Bert round for a drink and a chat, and to listen to a few of my recordings. He was impressed with some of the scores and said that he would fix the recording studio if I would fix the band. I decided to have an eight-piece outfit playing all my arrangements, with half the numbers being my own compositions. All the musicians I engaged had played with the top dance and swing bands, and Bert gave the group its name 'Billy Amstell's Dixie All-Stars'.

Whenever I had written a jazz number the problem had always been to decide on a title – that is, until it came into my mind to use the name of one of our cats! At one time we kept seven cats and eight in all are buried in the garden of our home. From Fifi, Happy Little Joe and Sue, Sue, I chose the latter for inclusion on the LP; and one of my earliest pieces, *Tootin' Around*, which I had recorded with both Ambrose and Jack Harris, just had to be included. After three sessions spread over two days we completed an album of 12 tracks, in which we tried to recreate some of the sounds we heard in the pre-war world of London after dark. Bert called the LP 'Session After Midnight'.

Reviewing the album in *Nostalgia* magazine, Peter Good wrote, '. . . *The Blues in B flat* serves as an introductory show-piece for each instrumentalist. I was reminded of Ted Lewis by some of Billy's playing . . . then Danny Moss blew on a lovely sounding tenor saxophone and Brian Lemon performed some nifty finger-work on the ivories. Billy Riddick, trumpet, and Ken Wood, trombone, also give more than a hint of other good sounds to follow. The restrained acoustic guitar of Ike Isaacs is also heard and Brian Emney on drums maintains an unobtrusive beat throughout the whole record (coming to the fore occasionally, I'm pleased to say) . . . As it was usual for any of the big jazz-players visiting London to sit-in on the late night "jam sessions", it is not surprising that influences of Duke Ellington, Garland Wilson, or Jimmy Dorsey can be detected . . . *Tootin' Around* . . . I could have willingly taken another two or three minutes of this! . . .'

Reviewing the record in *Jazz Journal*, Derrick Stewart-Baxter wrote, '. . . This LP presents some good arrangements of popular tunes and original compositions by Billy – including one dedicated to his cat, *Sue, Sue*, that wins my approval. He displays an acid, quirky tone on clarinet, the instrument he plays best, in my opinion. Tenor sax honours inevitably go to Danny Moss. Billy Riddick is another name from the past . . . he provides an adequate trumpet lead throughout. Brian Lemon once again shows just why he is so respected by his fellow musicians . . .'

Peter Good felt that we had captured the atmosphere of the 'Seamy Soho' clubs of the 1930s very accurately, but Derrick Stewart-Baxter disagreed . . . 'what we hear is nothing like an after midnight session in the clubs . . . fine music no doubt . . .' I must not forget that our lineup for the LP was completed by the dependable Art Learner on bass.

My other compositions on the record are *Paradise, Free 'n Easy*, and *Don't Fuss*, which became so named when, looking for a title as usual, I remembered the expression that Ambrose had used very often at rehearsals – 'Don't fuss, fellows, don't fuss'. In all I have had 30 numbers published. Many years ago I wrote two tunes in the Latin–American idiom (with lyrics by Ernie Bragg) which American publisher Jack Mills said had potential when he was over here in the early 1960s, and suggested that I contacted bandleader Edmundo Ros with a view to having them played over the radio. In that event, Jack said, he would consider publishing them. Having done a fair amount of work with Edmundo Ros, I knew him well enough to telephone his home. I was not sure I had heard him correctly when he quickly offered to 'plug' them over the air on a fifty-fifty basis. 'I beg your pardon,' I said. 'Half each,' he replied gruffly. I thought that was a bit greedy, so I said I would think it over; but after some consideration I decided not to phone him back. The result is that the manuscripts are in my piano stool to this day . . . On reflection, it would have been better to have had the tunes played and received half the royalties than get nothing at all! These two 'masterpieces' were the only numbers that I had ever written up to that time which were not in the jazz idiom.

At the end of January 1983, a Mr Norman Gardiner wrote to Alan Dell from the University of the South Pacific at Laucala Bay, Suva, Fiji, asking if I was still alive and requesting information about my career. He was also kind enough to give his opinion that I was 'the only English reedman who came near to the Americans – Freddy Gardner not excepted, and adding that 'he seems – so far as my books show – to have been an Ambrose man and nothing else.'

A copy of Mr Gardiner's letter was sent me by Brian Stephens, a producer of Alan Dell's 'Big Band Sound', who also wrote to Mr Gardiner assuring him that I was 'very much alive and well and still recording, as the enclosed album *Session After Midnight* will show.' I was greatly pleased – at least I had one fan somewhere in the world!

Rod Soar, of Pennine Radio and Radio Tees, told me in October 1984 that the album had been played quite a few times over local radio and also in exchange programmes with Harvey Lisker at Station W1BX in New York and with Tony Bretherick at Station 5MMM in Adelaide, Australia. Furthermore, Rod told me that he is working on an exchange with Wilf Lowe in Durban on behalf of the South African Broadcasting Corporation.

With all this publicity at my age, I really must remember my hat size.

33 Jewish Party

It was sometime in the early part of 1981 that I had the idea of recording an LP of Jewish party tunes that are also popular with non-Jewish people, so I mentioned it to Bert Wilcox, who agreed to arrange for the studio while I got the band together. I settled on a six-piece outfit, comprising, Neil Fullerton (t); Emilio (accordion); Art Learner (bass g); Harry Barnett (g); Brian Emney (d), and myself on clarinet. Oddly enough, although the music was Jewish, there was only one Jewish musician in the band. During the making of the record I recall saying to our singer, Lynn Collins, amid some laughter from the boys, 'Don't wave your arms about – people'll think you're Jewish!'

I thought it appropriate to space out the songs with some stories, typically Jewish in their humour, the obvious choice for telling them being that well known radio comic and TV entertainer, Harold Berens, who also acted as host. Most of the music comprised Yiddish folk songs that had come to this country from Eastern Europe with the Jews who had fled to the West from the tyranny which plagued Russia and Poland in the late nineteenth century.

I arranged all 15 tracks, which included ten traditional numbers and one of my own compositions, *Boobala* ('Grandma dear'). Among the most famous tunes on the record* are *Hava Nagila*, *Chasan Kallah Mazeltov*, *The Wedding Samba* and *Shalom Alachem*. The musicians achieved a splendid interpretation of the Yiddish folk songs, capturing the authentic spirit, while Lynn Collins, a Scots girl from Edinburgh, sang all her songs beautifully, including two in perfect Hebrew.

The record sleeve, with the traditional dancers, the blue and white sky and the menorah – loaned from the sideboard of our home – was inspired by Tessa, while I compiled the sleeve notes in which I explained the type and style of the music. It proved to be great fun editing and balancing the group on an eight-track recording machine; I was glad to be given an insight into this side of the business.

Family matters came very much to the forefront of my mind during the recording session. As we were making *Roszenkas Mit Mundel* ('Sleep, Baby, Sleep'), the memories came flooding back, for my 'booba' (paternal grandmother) had many times rocked me to sleep with this lullaby: nearly 70 years had passed since then! She it was who taught me Yiddish – at least I understand it, despite the fact that I do not speak it too well – and who lived to the ripe old age of 105! Her son, Morris, my father, died only six months after her, at the comparatively early age of 66. My dear mother, Sophie, lived to be 87. My brother Mick, the only

*Zodiac ZR1015.

128

other professional musician in the family, died in 1979, aged 78. I remember him as the idol of the family. Mick always spent everything he earned; but I, on the other hand, made it a rule early in life to save at least half of my earnings. Harry, my eldest brother, is also dead, but happily Sid and Alf are still alive; so is my sister Rose who gave me so much help early in my career. Sad to say, my eldest sister, Kitty, died when she was only 44. My earliest memories of Sid and Alf as young Boy Scouts remind me that I was once briefly a member of the Jewish Lads Brigade, and that when my mother saw me marching in a parade along Commercial Road in the East End of London, she burst into tears. Apparently she feared that I would be taken away for military service, as happened in Russia – and for a period of 25 years as had been my grandfather's unhappy lot. Because of her fear my mother insisted that I leave the organisation.

Tessa's family came to England from the West and not from the East like my own family. Her great-grandparents were among the first Jewish settlers in Hartford, Connecticut, where they were the founders of the *shul*. On Plymouth Hoe there stands a large statue of Queen Victoria, thought to have been placed there in her honour by Tessa's grandfather at the end of the nineteenth century.

Tessa's formal education was very different from mine for she was privately educated. She studied at the London College of Music, passing out with two silver medals – one for singing, the other for the violin. She also holds a gold medal for swimming.

As I have related in Chapter 12, Tessa and I were introduced to each other by Les Carew on the set at Pinewood Studios in 1937, when Ambrose and his Orchestra were featured in the film *Kicking the Moon Around*. The picture went out on general release in June 1938, the month in which Tessa and I were married.

Although it never set out to be so, the making of 'Jewish Party' was certainly a trip into nostalgia for me.

34 Yesterday, Today and Tomorrow

Into the 1980s and my own seventies, the dates have kept on coming. In the spring of 1982 I was involved in another exercise in nostalgia (deliberate this time) when I was invited, together with Tiny Winters, to take part in a Radio London programme devised by Bert Wilcox and called 'Way Up West Again'. With Bert, an acknowledged authority on the London dance band scene of the 1930s, at the wheel of his car, programme presenter David Carter with the recording equipment beside him, and Tiny and myself in the rear seats, we drove around the West End to some of the hotels and clubs where the bands were resident during the 'golden age of the dance bands'. Inevitably, in some cases redevelopment had changed the locations, often beyond recognition; but Bert's knowledge of the overall scene enabled him to establish where certain clubs and hotels had once stood. As we reached each spot he was able to tell the listeners which band was resident where and for how long during the late 1920s and the 1930s, illustrating his points by playing an appropriate record. Outside the May Fair Hotel and the Embassy Club I was brought in to chat about my own yesterdays. Could it really have been more than half a century since I first walked into the May Fair Hotel as a barely 20-year-old youngster? It seemed hardly credible.

Arriving in Old Compton Street at the site of the Queensbury Club – the pre-war London Casino where I had played with Jack Harris – I remembered being there in the war years with Geraldo's orchestra when Bing Crosby entertained the troops, accompanied only by a piano-accordionist.

Then in the autumn of 1982 I telephoned Roy Herbert, producer of the Radio 2 programme 'You and the Night and the Music', which went out during the week between 2am and 5am. I have known Roy since he joined the BBC at the age of 16, as a junior clerk at the Aeolian Hall Studios. 'How's about a broadcast?' I asked him, to which he replied: 'Why not!' 'Just like that?' I queried. 'Don't you want to hear me?' 'No,' he said. 'I know what you can do.'

So I formed a five-piece band, made up of: Brian Lemon (p); Brian Emney (d); Len Skeat (b); Dick Abel (g), plus myself on clarinet. We met at the Maida Vale Studios at 9.30am on 27 November. We finished at noon, having recorded eight titles – *Indiana*, *Rosetta*, *If I Had You*, *Blues in B flat*, *When You're Smiling*, *Autumn Leaves* (unaccompanied), *Liza* and *Don't Fuss*. The session was a success; we were all highly satisfied and the titles were aired over seven nights from 19 February 1983 and repeated from 19 April. The broadcasts were so well received that we were given a further session at the studios on 13 August, when we recorded another ten titles. I figured I must have been the most popular clarinet player, as far as the long distance lorry drivers were concerned anyway!

A few weeks after the November 1982 sessions, I approached the author and broadcaster Michael Freedland with an idea for his Sunday morning programme, 'You Don't Have to be Jewish' on Radio London. This was for a chat show, the first of its kind, featuring a number of prominent bandleaders and musicians. Michael liked the idea and asked me to assemble as many people as were available from the short list I had prepared. I succeeded in getting Stanley Black, Bert Firman, Harry Gold, Len Jackson, Ivor Mairants, Harry Smith, Alf van Straten and Nat Temple – plus, at Michael Freedland's express request, Joe Loss. As Stanley Black was not free to record the programme with the rest of us on 13 January, Michael arranged to pre-record his part at Stanley's home and then insert it into the show. The actual show, edited to fit into the 30-minute programme and interspersed with some records of the dance bands, was broadcast on 16 January 1983.

So great was the response that the two-hour unabridged version was broadcast at the end of January and a further compliment was paid when the edited programme was repeated on 19 June. As Tessa listened to the extended programme, she asked me: 'Why does everyone have to speak at the same time?' 'Because they're all Jewish!' I retorted, somewhat impatiently. A few days later I ran into my old friend, trumpeter Neil Fullerton: he told me he had tuned in to 'You Don't Have to be Jewish'. I couldn't help saying 'YOU don't have to be Jewish, but if you insist it could be painful!'

At the end of June I made a further appearance on Michael Freedland's show, when he interviewed that master of the *ad lib* Harold Berens, and myself, opening and closing the programmes with a track from the 'Jewish Party' album.

One day in November 1983 I came across the 'band engagements' book which I had maintained for nearly two and a half years during my time as Sergeant i/c the Station Dance Band and the Brass Band at RAF Wittering. Recorded in the book are the details of the bands' activities – dances and concerts both on and off the camp, church parades and marches, at squadron dances for 151, 266 and 25 Squadrons, at dispersal points and at boxing matches. All 40 years ago . . . ghosts from the past . . . inside the book a letter from The Stamford, Rutland and General Infirmary, of which I am especially proud, thanking the band for helping to raise the sum of £866 at the summer Carnival in 1942 . . .

As I turned it over I began to wonder if the RAF Central Band at Uxbridge would be interested in this book. I telephoned the Headquarters and was put through to Drum Major Terry McCarthy, whose name and rank were familiar to me – which was hardly surprising since it transpired that I had once known his late father, who had also been a Drum Major. Terry McCarthy promised that he would speak to Wing Commander Eric Banks, the current RAF Director of Music. He said he would telephone me in a couple of days, which he accordingly did, with an invitation for me to take all the information I had on the bands' engagements to show to his CO. So on 29 November I motored to Uxbridge with my precious book, numerous photographs, letters, programmes, etc. Little did they realise that I am a five-star hoarder!

On arrival at the camp two smart young airmen manning the barrier told me to report to the guardroom, now a modern building, so unlike the shack I had reported to more than 43 years ago. From there I was taken to the HQ office of the Central Band. On my way I noticed that the camp cinema, in which the famous RAF No 1 Dance Band, the Squadronaires, rehearsed during the war years, had been converted into a gymnasium, while the Central Band itself was now housed in a building of modern design. Wing Commander Banks, whose quiet and gentlemanly bearing so reminded me of the late Sid Phillips, chatted with me for an hour or so while the bandmaster, Warrant Officer Lambert, interested himself in all that I had brought along. I noted that what seemed to be of particular interest to the W/Cmdr were the Boxing programmes – one of which contained the name of Pilot Officer Len Harvey, then Heavyweight champion of Great Britain, who I had once watched box a four round exhibition bout with Aircraftsman Nash, Light Heavyweight Champion of the RAF, at the end of 1940. The boxing tournaments were greatly encouraged by all our COs.

Towards the end of our chat I felt very much at ease and, leaning forward in my chair, I asked the Director of Music, 'If I call you W/Cmdr, will you call me Sarge?' With a smile that again reminded me of Sid Phillips, he asked me if I would like two tickets for the next orchestral concert. He then promised to get in touch with me after he had arranged a meeting with F/Lt Kendrick, who was collating the activities of the five-piece bands which were sent out from Central Band HQ during the early years of the war. I could not help suggesting that maybe that was how we had won the war!

WO Lambert showed me round the various halls, in one of which I unexpectedly met Brian Hadden, a member of the Central Band, whose father, Sid Hadden, had been pianist/arranger when I was with Geoff Love's orchestra.

As WO Lambert showed me out he assured me that I would be welcome again any time,* while Brian Hadden** pressed me to have a drink with him sometime soon. Driving by the camp barrier I paused to look back at the old cookhouse – and at No 2 Block where I had cleaned out the latrines. More than 43 years had gone by . . . in the words of Sir Malcolm Sargent . . . 'in a flash'!

And so it goes on. The years may have passed but I am still busy in the job of making music. I play with my Quintet for broadcasting, for the 'Memory Lane' Jazz Festivals, for many other purposes – if that is the right word. Peter Boizot has given me dates at his Pizza Express restaurant in Dean Street, W1, and still does.

---

*As it happens, Tessa and I did go back to RAF Wittering for another visit on 30 August 1985, when we tied up a few more loose ends, did some things we had no time for before, and visited friends at Easton-on-the-Hill where we had lived during those old wartime days – and that made it 45 years!

**F/Sgt Brian Hadden was one of the 20 RAF bandsmen killed in the tragic accident when their coach smashed into the back of a fuel tanker on a German motorway near Munich on 11 February 1985.

It all keeps me going – and sometimes if I close my eyes it almost seems as if those years had never been and I am again a young lad sitting in the great Ambrose Orchestra of the 1930s. Even if it is not and cannot be so, I don't fuss either.

At the Memory Lane Party Night in London at the end of May 1985 I was both surprised and delighted to meet an old friend – delighted because it was Ray Sonin, Editor of *Melody Maker* from 1935 to 1956, and surprised since I knew he had been living in Canada for the past 20 years or more. There, in Toronto, he has his own weekly two and a half hour programme in which he features British jazz and British dance bands of the 1920s, 1930s and 1940s. During the evening Ray telephoned his radio station to give them news of the current London music scene.

So much for yesterday and today: what of tomorrow? I appear to have come full circle, by leaving the business the way I came into it. By that I mean that I started as a jazz musician and that's the way I am leaving. The intermediate years – playing sessions, radio and orchestral work – were nevertheless a wonderful experience. Tomorrow I shall practice the clarinet – as I have done today and did yesterday. I seldom play the tenor saxophone these days: it seems too heavy to carry around . . . or is it because I am pushing 75? I don't know whether either Benny Goodman or 'Peanuts' Hucko still have their own teeth, but my ever present fear is of losing mine! If this should happen, then I will stop playing and help Tessa with the hoovering!

Afterword

by Burnett James
Former Co-Editor *Jazz Journal*

Editing Billy Amstell's memoirs has been a particular pleasure for me, far beyond that of a publisher's normal duties. There is a specific reason. In the early days of 1935, after an active boyhood, I was struck down by a severe attack of paralytic polio and for the next two years I lay in a hospital bed, finding recompense as I could and where I could. Much of this came from listening to the radio and to what records I could obtain or cajole somebody into playing for me on a portable gramophone, for I could not manage even that for myself; and of course this was long before the days of hi-fi and remote controls. But now it all comes back to me vividly, if only because I soon discovered that my favourite band was, in fact, the great Ambrose orchestra of the mid-1930s of which Billy Amstell was a permanent member and a leading soloist. Apart from the records, it was those Saturday night broadcasts that did it; for despite hospital regulations I contrived to get my ear to my bedside radio without provoking protest or complaint.

Reading through the pages of *Don't Fuss, Mr Ambrose* brings back both contemporary memories and generates a few later thoughts. I am intrigued by much of what Billy Amstell says, and I am particularly taken with his reminder of how Mr Ambrose used to sniff whenever new men entered the ranks and mutter, 'I wish I hadn't changed the band!' Disconcerting for the newcomers, obviously – but not only for them. Fans hate change too. I was no exception. I remember my distress when the trombone trio of Lew Davis, Ted Heath and Tony Thorpe broke up, even though the ultimate in disaster was averted because the premier member, Lew Davis (to my mind the finest of all the Ambrose soloists – pardon Billy!), remained and the replacements ensured no decline in standards. But it seemed then as though the change – any change – must be for the worse, even if it was not; an unwarranted and unnecessary disturbance of the order of things as they are and should be.

Being reminded of the Ambrose band of those days, and hearing the records again, some of them after more than 30 years, I am impressed anew by both the ensemble work and by the soloists. I have by force of circumstance always been a listener rather than a dancer, although but for illness I am sure I would have danced out both my shoes with the best. For this reason I was and have remained particularly attracted to the jazz numbers the band regularly featured, especially those charted by Sid Phillips; an addiction to the music of Duke Ellington forged a common linkage, though not in my own case until a little later.

I have long thought that the Ambrose band of the mid-1930s was every bit as good as the Glenn Miller USAAF band that attained such exaggerated popularity only a few years later, and possessed better soloists. (Where, outside Ellington and one or two of the top black American bands, could be found a *better* front line quartet of soloists than Max Goldberg, Lew Davis, Danny Polo and Billy Amstell?). But because it was caught up in and by the demands of commercial dance music – designed to appeal directly to the society set who seldom *listened* to anything – its fullest potential was perhaps never quite realised.

If I have a specific criticism to make of the Ambrose band today, it is that it tended to play too fast and too staccato. But that was really more a failing of the period and its social ambience than of the band itself. It was an age of rather hectic staccato playing, at least when anything of a 'jazz' nature was purveyed, presumably under the popular illusion that 'hot' was (and often still is) regarded as synonymous with fast, furious, and noisy.   (Ironically one of Ambrose's pet hates was 'loud noise'.)

The conductor Wilhelm Furtwängler used to insist that the art of interpretation consisted primarily in finding the right tempo. Very much the same applies to popular music. Of course it does not end with tempo alone, at least with tempo in the abstract; but it does surface as a first principle. How many times has an otherwise good performance been ruined by a tempo at obvious variance with the basic material? – how many 'standard' tunes as well as 'originals' have suffered total distortion because of lack of sensitivity to this essential point? Ambrose did not always avoid the pitfall. One example is *B'Wanga*, an excellent Sid Phillips number in something like the Ellington 'jungle' style. It was a great favourite of mine (perhaps I was particularly taken by the title); but I was shocked, when hearing it again all these years later, to find how the over-fast tempo, and therefore the essential 'body-movement', conflicted with the structure, both melodic and harmonic, even though Phillips himself must have had a hand in the performance. I had preserved it in my mind as around 25% slower; and I am convinced it would sound better that way.

But, as I say, that was all as much a matter of period convention as of individual selection. The habit of playing fast and furious in that clipped staccato style too often meant that the music was fundamentally un- or non-rhythmic. For rhythm is not what happens on the beat, but what goes on between the beat. If nothing interesting happens between the beat, there is not real rhythm (and certainly no 'swing'), and no amount of talk about 'rhythmic music' can make up for the deficiency. The Ambrose band was a good deal better than most of the period in this respect, but the conventions of the time again too often frustrated it. The nearer it (or any other band) came to the true jazz idiom, the more genuinely 'rhythmic' it became. All the same, the convention tended to insist that quick staccato spelt 'hot', regardless of . . .' as old Sir Henry Wood used to say.

And what of Billy Amstell himself? He exchanged chairs in the Ambrose reed section with Joe Jeannette in the early 1930s and thereafter took all the tenor solos, becoming in the process one of the band's most distinctive voices. Listening now I discern a number of lines of development that were perhaps not so easy to define or analyse at the time. This was the period when the tenor saxophone was still dominated by the big-toned, big-boned style of Coleman Hawkins. Billy was not in this respect a Hawkins follower, though he was certainly a Hawkins admirer. His tone was lighter, airier, more sinuous than that of the typical adherents of the Hawkins school. For Billy Amstell started out on alto saxophone before switching to tenor, and his tone and general approach were certainly influenced by his beginnings. He was by no means the only one: the interaction of alto and tenor in the formation of a number of saxophone styles is a subject worth detailed examination and analysis. It ranges in several different directions. In his early days, especially when he joined the Fletcher Henderson orchestra as replacement for Coleman Hawkins, and before his own style was recognised let alone accepted, the other reedmen kept telling Lester Young that he ought to be playing alto, because of his light fragile (as it then seemed) tone. In fact one of Lester's primary influences was Frankie Trumbauer, who played that curious hybrid pitched between alto and tenor known as the C-melody saxophone. And Ben Webster, after being dubbed a Hawkins 'imitator' for years and becoming irked by it, ultimately evolved a unique style by blending the big Hawkins sound in the lower and middle ranges with the tonal and lyric grace of Johnny Hodges higher up. Billy Amstell never sounded like Coleman Hawkins or Ben Webster, least of all like Lester Young, although the tonal ambience of his style was more in that line than the other. I detect in some of Billy's solos a few echoes of Eddie Miller, even a hint here and there of Bud Freeman, though Billy's tone was never asthmatic like Bud's. In general, however, his style and tone were his own, his voice individual.

Inevitably one remembers him principally in those Ambrose years, for although he played later with many other bands, including those of Geraldo and Stanley Black, his most distinctive years as a jazz tenor player and band soloist were those with Ambrose between 1931 and 1940. And of course Billy was (and is) at heart always a 'jazzer', a devotee of what the French persist in calling *'le jazz hot'*. Like many such he found the routine of churning out commercial dance music night

136

after night somewhat wearisome, though he carried it out loyally enough, at least until after the immediate post-war years.

His nimble clarinet playing, preserved into his seventies and mindful always of the beneficient influence of Danny Polo, beside whom he sat in the Ambrose ranks came to him originally via Jimmy Dorsey and Benny Goodman, Dorsey in particular. It was Jimmy Dorsey's alto playing which struck deep into him in the days of his nonage, and I am sure that it, as well as the Dorsey clarinet, percolated through into the mix and blend of his tenor evolutions. It was perhaps the predominant early influence. To hear Billy Amstell playing tenor saxophone with Ambrose defines the provenance: as well as a detectable gutsy quality in the belly of the instrument, and a kind of Dorsey-like elegance of line and delineation above, there is a certain impish implication all through – which reflects himself very accurately. It is present in his memoirs too: the style is the man.

As a last thought, I am amused by the way Billy says, or has said elsewhere, that he did not realise how good the Ambrose band was at the time but only came to recognise it much later by hearing the reissued records by other bands. That, I am sure, is something to be taken with a fistful of the old Siberian mineral. They were proud men, those Ambrosians; they were good, they knew they were good, and they meant to be good – Bert Ambrose himself not least. They may not have shouted it from the rooftops: they didn't need to; they had only to play. Half a century later it seems incontrovertable. The best band in the land, and Billy Amstell was an essential ingredient of it.

He is a survivor too; and at a time when too many of his generation are falling or have fallen, Billy Amstell, with his ever active clarinet (the instrument once given to him by Danny Polo), reminds us that Father Time really can be told to stand in the corner and not speak until spoken to.

Appendix

Personnel of the 'augmented' Ambrose Orchestra that played the Royal Opera House on 30 June 1935. (*) indicates permanent member of the Ambrose orchestra at the time.

DANNY POLO (*) (as, cl)
Played with most important leaders in US; learned clarinet before taking up saxophone; leader of reed section and principal clarinet soloist.

JOE JEANNETTE (*) (as)
Studied clarinet both at Royal Academy of Music and Kneller Hall, under Charles Draper; also played flute; second alto in band.

BILLY AMSTELL (*) (ts, cl)
'A facile performer on tenor and clarinet . . . outstanding ability as clarinet player first attracted attention . . . developed individual style on tenor saxophone . . .' (Programme notes).

SID PHILLIPS (*) (bar, cl)
Studied all branches of music in various Continental conservatoires; outstanding composer and arranger.

MAX GOLDBERG (*) (t)
Born in London but raised in Canada; first learnt French horn; pastmaster in the use of mutes; phenomenal microphone technique.

HARRY OWEN (*) (t)
Learned trumpet in the Army; changed to clarinet for eight years; returned to study trumpet under Charles Ancliffe.

BILLY FARRELL (t)
Also an excellent performer on piano, piano-accordion and violin.

LEW DAVIS (*) (tb)
Noted for beautiful tone; advanced rhythmic player; complete mastery of instrument; adept in use of mutes to produce novel tone colours.

TED HEATH (*) (tb)
Began playing tenor horn in brass band at age seven; possibly best British exponent of Negro style of playing. Famous bandleader in own right in later years.

TONY THORPE (*) (tb)
Played with leading Canadian and American bands before arriving in England

in 1926. Unusual method of vibrato produced from throat not by moving slide.

ERIC SIDDAY (vln)

Former Royal Academy student; advanced rhythmic player; also orchestrator, composer and conductor.

REG LEOPOLD (vln)

Took Licentiate's diploma at Trinity at 18; noted for good tone and technical ability.

REG PURSGLOVE (vln)

Entered Guildhall School of Music and won Carnegie Scholarship.

ERNIE LEWIS (vln)

Won Sassoon Scholarship five years in succession; member of symphony orchestra at 13.

HUGO RIGNOLD (vln)

Master of both classical and jazz music; former student of Royal Academy.

BERT BARNES (*) (p)

Brilliant pianist; arranger of great merit; had arranged for all principal bands.

JOE BRANNELLY (*) (g)

Former banjoist in US Navy Jazz Band; used specially tuned four stringed guitar in preference to usual six stringed g.

DICK BALL (*) (b)

Outstanding rhythmic performer on double bass; started playing at 15.

MAX BACON (*) (d)

One of finest swing drummers in the world; artistic cymbal player; special fondness for exotic rumba rhythms.

CHARLIE BOTTERILL (perc)

Began musical career as violinist; became fascinated by tympani and drums.

ARTHUR YOUNG (p)

Featured piano soloist; played his concerto *Thames Rhapsody*.

and vocalists –

ELSIE CARLISLE (*); JACK COOPER (*); DONALD STEWART; The Rhythm Sisters (KAY MUNRO-SMITH; HELEN RAYMOND; JEAN CONIBEAR); The Rhythm Brothers (CLIVE ERARD; RONNIE HILL; JACK LORRIMER).

Abbreviations

Key to instrumental abbreviations, both here and throughout the book:
(t) trumpet; (tb) trombone; (as) alto saxophone; (ts) tenor saxophone; (bar) baritone saxophone; (cl) clarinet; (fl) flute; (vln) violin; (p) piano; (b) string bass; (d) drums; (perc) percussion; (g) guitar.

Discography

DON'T FUSS MR AMBROSE
A double album issued by Decca to celebrate the publication of this book and featuring Billy Amstell's work with various bands, but principally that of Bert Ambrose between 1930 and 1939. The titles are arranged in chronological order; after each title in the following listing the name of the band appears in brackets with the name of the vocalist, if any, and the date of the original recording, thus: Nevertheless (*Ambrose/Sam Browne – 16.9.1931*). Further details can be found on the album sleeve.

Side 1:
You Brought a New Kind of Love (*Jack Harris/voc unknown – 5.7.1930*); The Moon is Low (*Jack Harris/voc unknown – 16.7.1930*); A Peach of a Pair (*Roy Fox/Al Bowlly – 28.1.1931*); I'm So Used To You Now (*Roy Fox/Al Bowlly – 1.6.1931*); Leave the Rest to Nature (*Roy Fox/Al Bowlly – 1.6.1931*); Swanee (*Stanley Black – 11.9.1931*); I Ain't Got Nobody (*Stanley Black/Nat Gonella – 11.9.1931*); Nevertheless (*Ambrose/Sam Browne – 16.9.1931*; When We're Alone (*The Blue Mountaineers/Sam Browne – 17.5.1932*)

Side 2:
Sweet Sixteen and Never Been Kissed (*Blue Mountaineers/Sam Browne & Nat Gonella – 11.9.1932*); My Romance (*Ambrose/Sam Browne – 27.10.1932*); The Old Man of the Mountain (*Doris Hare/accomp. – 2.11.1932*); La-di-da-di-da (*Ambrose/Sam Browne – 30.11.1933*); Without That Certain Thing (*Elsie Carlisle/accomp. – 20.1.1934*); The Very Thought of You (*Ambrose/Sam Browne – 11.5.1934*); La Cucaracha (*Ambrose/Sam Browne – 24.10.1934*); Okay, Toots (*Ambrose/The Rhythm Sisters – 5.12.1934*); Hitchy Koo (*Embassy Eight – 1.2.1935*)

Side 3:
He's a Rag Picker (*Embassy Eight – 1.2.1935*); Streamline Strut (*Ambrose – 20.3.1935*); B'Wanga (*Ambrose – 15.4.1935*); St Louis Blues (*Louis de Vries – 5.6.1935*); Moonglow (*Louis de Vries/Brian Lawrence – 5.6.1935*); Life Begins When You're in Love (*Ambrose/Jack Cooper – 20.3.1936*); Hide and Seek (*Ambrose – 29.6.1936*); Organ Grinder's Swing (*Ambrose/Evelyn Dall – 14.10.1936*; Tarantula (*Ambrose – 30.12.1936*)

Side 4:
Power House *(Ambrose – 27.7.1937)*; Swing is in the Air *(Ambrose/Evelyn Dall – 24.3.1937)*; Mr Reynard's Nightmare *(Ambrose – 10.2.1939)*; Voodoo *(Ambrose – 10.2.1939)*; Tootin' Around *(Ambrose–Amstell 10.2.1939)*; Beer Barrel Polka *(Ambrose/Evelyn Dall – 7.7.1939)*; The Penguin *(Ambrose – 17.6.1939)*; The War Dance of the Wooden Indians *(Ambrose – 13.6.1939)*; If A Grey-Haired Lady Says 'How's Yer Father?' *(Ambrose/Jack Cooper – 27.11.1939)*

Decca RFLD51

SESSION AFTER MIDNIGHT
Blues in B flat; The British Grenadiers; Tishomingo Blues; Paradise; Free 'n Easy; Don't Fuss/Washington and Lee Swing; Tootin' Around; My Old Kentucky Home; Sue Sue (My Cat); My Bonnie is Over the Ocean; Royal Garden Blues.

Billy Amstell's Dixie All Stars
Billy Amstell (cl, ts); Bill Riddick (t); Ken Woods (tb); Danny Moss (ts); Brian Lemon (p); Brian Emney (d); Art Learner (b); Ike Isaacs (g).

Zodiac London Jazz Classics 1010, stereo TS8014

BILLY AMSTELL'S JEWISH PARTY WITH HAROLD BERENS
Tonight's the Night; Tzena Tzena Tzena; Hava Nagila; Boobala (Grandma Dear); Shah Shah Der Rebba Geyt; Der Broyges Tanz; Wedding Samba/Chasan Kallah Mazeltov; Sleep Baby Sleep (Roszenkas mit mundel); Vos Bist Du Catsala Broyges; A Freilache Tanz; Kazatska; David; Ich bin a Boarder bay mein Weib; Shalom Alachem.
Billy Amstell (cl); Neil Fullerton (t); Emilio (accordion); Brian Emney (d); Art Learner (b); Harry Barnett (g); Lynn Collins (vcl); Harold Berens, host.

Zodiac ZR1015

Index

Aaronson, Abe 21
Abbet, Leon 18
Adam, Paul 92
Adorée, Renée 15
Allen, Nat 84, 91
Ambrose, Bert (and
    Orchestra) 27ff, 57, 67,
    69, 76, 78–81, 83, 85, 88,
    92, 93, 94, 96, 105, 111,
    116–117 (death), 119,
    134–137, 138
Amstell, Mick (brother) 11,
    12, 15, 17, 18, 19, 21, 26,
    27, 59, 128–129
Amstell, Rose (sister) 11,
    12, 129
Amstell, Harry (brother) 11,
    129
Amstell, Kitty (sister) ii, 12,
    129
Amstell, Sid (brother) 11,
    13, 15, 23, 129
Amstell, Tessa (wife) 50, *et
    seq.*
Armstrong, Louis 45, 103
Ashley, Lady Sylvia 38
Astor, Lady 52
Aspiazu, Don 34, 37

Bacon, Max 27, 29, 34,
    44–46, 49, 55, 138
Bain, Jock 70, 76
'Bag 'O'Nails', The 27, 31
Baker, Josephine 49
Baker, Kenny 59, 95
Ball, Dick 138
Ball, Kenny 117–118
Banks, W/Cmdr. 131, 132
Barber, Chris 39
Barnes, Bert 38, 43–44, 48,
    138
Barley, Neville 11, 13
Barretto, Don 48

Beiderbecke, Bix 32, 35
Berens, Harold 128
Berigan, Bunny 25
Berly, Harry 26–28
Bentine, Michael 89,
    113–114
Bianci, Marcel 80
Bidgood, Harry 37
Binney, Don 25
Black, Stanley, OBE 25,
    84ff, 92, 98ff, 101, 120,
    131
Bluitt, Kitty 87
Boizot, Peter 132
Boosey & Hawkes 60, 84,
    108
Boswell, Connie 40–41
Bowlly, Al 21, 26–28
Bradley, Buddy 30
Brannelly, Joe 25, 29, 30,
    32, 36, 37, 46, 49, 110,
    116, 138
Breeze, Eric 45, 51, 54, 56,
    67
Brisson, Carl 26*n*
Broadhurst, (Sir) Harry 58
Browne, Sam 29, 31, 32, 35,
    38, 40, 48, 52, 110
Brunis, George 25
Buchel, Philip 18
Buckman, Sid 26
Bullimore, Bert 59, 86, 88,
    98
Burman, Maurice 38,
    68–71, 72, 73, 75, 88, 97
Busse, Henry 15
Byng, Douglas 27

Caesar, Sid 101–102
Calloway, Cab 39
Calvert, Eddie 86
Camber, Len 70, 71, 73
Canberra, SS 119–121

Carew, Les 48, 50, 51, 81,
    129
Carlisle, Elsie 31, 32, 37, 38,
    39, 43, 139
Carmichael, Hoagy 31–32
Carr, Pearl 104–105
Carroll, Madeleine 41
Chaplin, Charlie 69, 106
Chequers Dance Band 11
Chevalier, Maurice 100
Chisholm, George 15, 67,
    91, 102–103, 106–107
Chiltern, Charles 91
Christian, Emile 34
Churchill, (Sir) Winston 65,
    113
Ciro's Club 47, 48, 68,
    78–81, 82–83, 84, 85, 92,
    93
Collins, Lynn 128
Collier, Jack, 75
Cooper, Jack 139
Cotton, Billy 26, 64
Cooper, Gladys 41
Costa, Sam 86
Coupland, Diana 98, 99
Crossman, Joe 11, 29, 30,
    31, 34, 35, 52, 81, 96
Cugat, Xavier 34
Cummings, Jock 67

D'Arcy, Bertram 13, 14
D'Arcy's Band 12, 14, 15
Dall, Evelyn 43, 45, 51–52
Dandridge, Dorothy 88
Daniels, Bebe 87, 88, 94
Darewski, Herman 17, 18
Davis, Ben 24
Davis, Beryl 25
Davis, Bobby 18, 20
Davis, Lew 26, 38, 45,
    134–135, 138
Dawn, Julie 73, 74

Dell, Alan, 11, 123, 126–127
Dennis, Denny 52
Desmond, Florence 50
Dessary, André 39
Diamond, Hughie 54, 55
Dorsey Brothers 20, 36, 89
Dorsey, Jimmy 18, 24–25, 30, 40, 94, 126, 137
Dorsey, Tommy 40
Duchin, Eddie 47

Echian, André 49
Edgerton, Col. 41–42
Edward, Prince of Wales 35, 38–41
Ellington, Duke 37, 47, 95, 126, 134–135
Ellington, Ray 57
Elizalde, Fred 18
Elrick, George 43
Embassy Club 21, 29, 38ff, 58, 78, 130
Embry, W/Cmdr. (later Air Marshal Sir) Basil 60, 62–63
Erard, Clive 15

Farley, Max 18, 20
Ferrie, Joe 28
Ffrench, Clinton 45, 67
Flemming, Jock 21
Foster, Teddy 45
Foy, Eddie 39
Fox, Roy 21, 26, 28, 38, 52, 56, 119
Frank, Aubrey 59, 68, 81, 101
Frankel, Ben 26, 105
Freeland, Michael 11, 131
Freeman, Bud 136
Fryer, Alec 20
Fullerton, Neil 110, 122, 131

Garby, Professor 110–111
Gardner, Freddy 91
Gaskin, Lud 34
Gee, Tessa (see under Amstell – wife) 50
Geraldo 38, 68, 69, 70, 71, 76, 77, 88, 100, 105

Gerhardi, Bill 21–23
Getz, Stan 108–109
Gibbons, Carroll 30, 64
Gillispie, Dizzy 47
Gillis, Burton 22
Glover, Bill 84, 86, 88
Goehr, Walter 83
Gold, Harry 88, 95, 131
Gold, Laurie 88–89
Goldberg, Max 26, 29, 35, 39, 51, 52, 54, 135, 138
Gonella, Nat 26, 28, 85
Goodman, Benny 20, 21, 36, 47, 58, 89, 92, 93, 94, 95, 99, 123, 124, 133, 137
Gorman, Ross 15
Granz, Norman 96
Green, Harry 17
Green, Johnny 70, 72

Hadden, F/Sgt. 132
Hall, Adelaide 53
Hall, Henry 22, 38, 43, 89
Hare, Doris 26n
Harris, Albert 48, 49
Harris, Jack 21, 23, 47, 53, 54, 64, 84, 130
Harris, Marion 35
Harty, Bill 21, 26
Hawkins, Coleman 136
Hayes, Harry 20, 37
Hayes, Patricia 87
Hayes, Tubby 93
Hayworth, Rita 78
Heath, Ted 29, 30, 35, 37, 38, 71, 72, 74, 83, 95, 134–135, 138
Heiger, Sid 56, 58, 91, 121–122
Helfer, Johnny 32
Herbert, Roy 11, 130
Hill, Teddy 47
Hilda, Bernard 93, 95
Hobson, Valerie 87
Hodges, Johnny 136
Holloway, Stanley 19
Horne, Kenneth 86, 87
Hucko, 'Peanuts' 7, 8, 69, 93, 94, 118, 123–124, 133
Hughes, Spike 24, 26, 33
Hunter, Harry, 86n, 87, 90
Hutton, Barbara 38

Hylton, Jack 50, 105, 114

Ivy, Claude 24

Jacobs, David 84
Jacobs, Howard 32
Jackson, Jack 104
Jaffa, Max 54, 64, 118
Jeanette, Joe 28, 31, 36, 41, 116
Johnson, Teddy 104–105
Jones, Ken 99

Kahn, Prince Aly 41, 80
Kahn, Harry 110, 118, 121
Kaye, Dave 21
Keel, Howard 105
Kemp, Hal 25
Kent, Duke of 51
Kenton, Stan 105
Kinsman, Tommy 37, 92, 110, 112–115
Kit-Kat Club 15, 19, 24
Knight, Peter 105–106
Kunz, Charlie 15

Lally, Arthur 49
Lang, Eddie 24
Levis, Carol 86
Lewis, Harry 67
Lewis, Ted 24
Lillie, Beatrice 49
Logan, Ella 32
Lombardo, Guy 37
London Casino 54, 84
Loss, Joe 131
Love, Geoff 101, 105, 120
Lynn, Vera 52, 99, 102, 104
Lyon, Ben 87, 94

McCaffer, Don 45
McQuater, Tommy 15, 48, 51, 67, 106, 117
McKinley, Ray 69
Mairants, Ivor 52, 71, 73, 131
Mastrem, Carmen 76
May Fair Hotel, 27ff, 47, 55, 57, 58, 60, 114, 130
Merrick, Mrs Kate, 18, 113
Miller, Eddie 136
Miller, Glenn 68–70, 76, 77, 118, 123, 124, 134

Milligan, Spike 57, 89–90, 102–103
Monseigneur Restaurant 26, 31, 119
Montgomery, Field Marshal 71, 73
Moss, Danny 126
Mouncey, Arthur 56, 59, 66, 79, 91
Murdoch, Richard 'Stinker' 86

Nathan, Jack 56, 119
Niblo, Arthur 21, 26
Noble, Ray 29
Norman, Monty 98, 99

Oliver, Vic 49, 94
Oronsay, SS 110–111, 121
Owen, Harry 32

Parker, Charlie 96–97
Payne, Jack 15, 59, 84, 98, 105
Payne, Norman 18, 20
Peck, Nat 124
Peterson, Oscar 93
Phillips, Sid 32, 38, 45, 49, 50, 54, 83, 95, 105, 117–118, 132, 134–135
Pogson, E.O. (Poggy) 54
Pollack, Ben 20, 36
Polo, Danny 31, 34, 36, 39, 52, 83, 94, 106, 108, 137, 138
Prendergast, Gene 34

Rabin, Oscar 15, 25
Race, Steve 86, 105
Radio Shows –
  'Bernard Braden Show' 86
  'Black and White Minstrel Show' 106
  'The Goon Show' 86, 113
  'High Gang' 94
  'Life With the Lyons' 86, 87
  'Much Binding in the Marsh' 86
  'Ray's a Laugh', 86, 87
  'Top Score' 86

'Up the Pole' 86
Read, Bert 29, 32, 35, 37
Rignold, Hugo 22, 139
Ritte, Ernest 26–27
Robinson, Eric 105, 120
Robinson, Stanford 92
Rollini, Adrian 18
Ros, Edmundo 126
Rosaire, Carmen 107
Rose, David 88
Ross, Annie 33
Roy, Harry 21, 78, 85, 96

Sargent, Sir Malcolm 79
Scott, Ronnie 93, 108–109
Scott-Wood, George 40
Sellers, Peter 89–90
Senter, Boyd 24
Shadwell, Charles 85
Sharon, Ralph 88, 95, 96
Shaw, Artie 102, 124
Shelton, Anne 79, 104
Sherman, Harry 27
Shields, Jack 32
Simmons, Lou 27
Skinner, Sgt. 'Ginger' 66–67, 74
Sonin, Ray 132
Spanier, Muggsy 25
Squadronaires 67, 70
Stapleton, Cyril 90, 98
Stevens, F/Lt. 'Cats Eye' 63, 64–65
Stewart, Johnny 86
Stewart-Baxter, Derrick 126
Stone, Lew 26–27, 31, 36, 57, 91, 92
Stutely, Don 26, 33, 47

Teagarden, Jack 94
Temple, Nat 131
Ternent, Billy 94
Thorpe, Tony 38, 138
Thornhill, Claude 94
Trenchard, Lord 60
Tucker, Sophie 15

Vallee, Rudy 30, 79
Ventura, Ray 39, 49, 94
Vries, Loius de 26n, 92

Waller, Thomas 'Fats' 53

Walters, Abe 78
Watson, Charles, 19–20
Wearsma, Melle 92
Weber, Marek 39
Wellington, Duke of 38
Whiteman, Paul 14, 16, 47, 55
Wilcox, Bert 95, 128, 130
Winnick, Maurice 26, 59, 68, 92, 95
Winters, Tiny 48, 51, 56, 91
Withers, Googie 30